FINDING

Hope

IN THE

VALLEYS

OF LIFE

FINDING
Hope
IN THE
VALLEYS
OF LIFE

MARY
THRASHER

MOODY PRESS
CHICAGO

© 2002 by
MARY THRASHER

All Scripture quotations, unless otherwise indicated, are taken from the *Holy Bible, New International Version*®. NIV®. Copyright © 1973, 1978, 1984 by International Bible Society. Used by permission of Zondervan Publishing House. All rights reserved.

Scripture quotations marked NKJV are taken from the *New King James Version.* Copyright © 1979, 1980, 1982 by Thomas Nelson, Inc. Used by permission. All rights reserved.

Scripture quotations marked KJV are taken from the King James Version.

Scripture quotations marked NASB are taken from the *New American Standard Bible*®, Copyright © The Lockman Foundation 1960, 1962, 1963, 1968, 1971, 1972, 1973, 1975, 1977, 1995. Used by permission.

Scripture quotations marked NLT are taken from the *Holy Bible, New Living Translation,* copyright © 1996. Used by permission of Tyndale House Publishers, Inc., Wheaton, Illinois 60189. All rights reserved.

Scripture quotations marked RSV are from the *Revised Standard Version* of the Bible, copyright 1946, 1952, and 1971 by the Division of Christian Education of the National Council of the Churches of Christ in the USA. Used by permission. All rights reserved.

Library of Congress Cataloging-in-Publication Data

Thrasher, Mary.
    Finding hope in the valleys of life / Mary Thrasher.
      p. cm.
    ISBN 0-8024-2249-7
    1. Christian life--Meditations. 2. Hope--Religious aspects--Christianity --Meditations. I. Title.

BV4501.3 .T49 2002
248.8'6--dc21

2002019884

1 3 5 7 9 10 8 6 4 2

Printed in the United States of America

To Bill,
Whose unending encouragement has been my inspiration,
Whose unfailing prayers have been my strength,
Whose unconditional love has been my haven.
God has blessed above and beyond
whatever I could have asked.

CONTENTS

Part 3
VALLEYS OF THE HEART

ACKNOWLEDGMENTS

$\mathcal{G}$od always gives to us in abundance—His surprises are always extra icing on the cake. Like the title of C. S. Lewis's book expresses, we are *Surprised by Joy.* A great surprise of joy for me has been the opportunity and privilege to write this book. To those who have made this possible, I am deeply grateful.

Special thanks goes to Elsa Mazon, who astounded me with the suggestion that I write a book. Little did she know this idea had been "on the shelf" for a number of years. Her interest brought the idea back to life. Sincere gratitude goes to Greg Thornton, whose godly words of encouragement were such a great "lifter of my spirit." To Cheryl Dunlop, whose careful eye helped in so many ways to make the manuscript more readable, goes my deep appreciation. I am grateful also to the members of my family with whom I have walked and whose valleys I have detailed in the book, as well as to friends who have shared their sorrows with me and desired others to know the good God who has helped them. I am also thankful for the many others from whose lives I have gleaned such wonderful stories of God's faithfulness.

My children have been such a wonderful source of encouragement that the Lord has provided. And my special love, my husband Bill, took the small seed of an idea and carefully, prayerfully, and sometimes painfully tended that seed until it bore fruit. Thank you, my dearest, for your wise suggestions, your encouragement, your sacrifice, and, most of all, your love.

Indeed, words are inadequate to express my humble thanks and greatest praise to my Maker and Lord, whose guiding hand has led me each moment through the peaks and valleys of my life. Great is Thy faithfulness.

INTRODUCTION

The rainbow is a symbol of God's faithfulness—His reminder to people of His promise to Noah never again to destroy the earth with water. After the storms the rainbow garners its lovely colors from refractions of the sun through raindrops. The believer's life also symbolizes God's faithfulness—the lovely tints in our lives mirror the goodness of a great Sovereign. And, as with the storms of nature, times of trial will one day cease.

As we are reminded of His faithfulness, God is also constantly reminding us of our status as pilgrims in this journey of life. Knowing God does not exclude the trials of life. Quite the opposite is true. Life on this earth, because of sin, is wrought with many sighs and heartaches. The question is not *if* we will suffer but *when.* As we enter each valley, the way in which we meet the shadows will determine our walk through it.

Noah's ark was a haven of God for him and his family during the Flood. God is still that haven of rest and safety for His children when all the world is dark and cold. As the dove returned to the ark when she could find no place to rest her feet, Noah reached out and brought the dove back into the ark to himself. As His children are wearied with life's sorrows, so God always reaches out and brings us back to Himself, our haven.

We each go through various valleys of affliction. James 1:2 tells us to "consider it all joy, my brethren, when you encounter various trials" (NASB). Like the rainbow those trials are multicolored, various. In 1 Peter 4:10, the word *various* is employed to express God's multifaceted grace. He always provides the matching grace we need for each specific difficulty we encounter. Our loving Father has not left us to bear our troubles and sorrows alone. He does not delight in our suffering, but He does delight in the finished product of our refinement. That is what suffering accomplishes in us—a grace distinguishable from the rest of the world. God produces an abundant grace within us that we could not acquire had we not been subjected to hardship.

In his *Letters to Malcolm,* C. S. Lewis wrote,

We—or at least I—shall not be able to adore God on the highest occasions if we have learned no habit of doing so on the lowest. . . . Any patch of sunlight in a wood will show you something about the sun which you could never get from reading books on astronomy. These pure and spontaneous pleasures are "patches of Godlight" in the woods of our experience.[1]

How does a child of God experience joy in the midst of a valley? By viewing not the darkness of the hour but the Godlight on the horizon.

Many verses in the Bible give us the confidence that "we know," not that we understand all, but we *know* the One who has ordered our lives so that "in all things [He] works for the good of those who love [Him]"—even the worst of life, of sins, of sickness or failure, of disappointment and fears. None of the various hues of suffering are left uncovered; all are covered by His grace and His constant attention.

When we reach our heavenly resting place, our trials will be remembered no more. What God has prepared for us is beyond our comprehension. All tears, all burdens will be vanquished. In this life, we believers are clothed with the mantle of Christ, His suffering as well as His righteousness. And in eternity we will share in the victory He purchased for us, a "priceless inheritance . . . kept in heaven for you, pure and undefiled, beyond the reach of change and decay" (1 Peter 1:4 NLT).

This book is not intended to offer simple explanations or solutions to suffering; there are none. I have attempted to deal with common issues that are familiar to most people, not only difficult matters such as death but everyday issues that most of us will face at one time or another. It would be helpful for you go through the Table of Contents to see which subjects fit your particular need, or the need of someone you know. The most important thing I want the reader to focus on is the Word of God, for within its covers you will find solace to meet every heartache.

In my own life I have been faced with many of the issues I have written about, or I have been closely associated with those who were going through these difficult times. I have brought personal examples into many of the topics and in all those situations I can testify to God's faithfulness.

This book was born of a deep desire to give consolation to troubled and burdened hearts, to help those who are struggling with different "hues" of suffering, within different valleys, to focus on the One who is the God of all comfort. The apostle Paul expressed in his letter to the Corinthians, "That is why, for Christ's sake, I delight in weaknesses, in insults, in hardships, in persecutions, in difficulties. For when I am weak, then I am strong" (2 Corinthians 12:10).

I encourage you to be strong in the Lord and in the power of His might. It is my prayer that as you pass through your valley, you will allow the colors of God's rainbow to shine brightly in your weakness, bringing strength to your soul and honor to your Maker.

NOTE

1. C. S. Lewis, *Letters to Malcolm, Chiefly on Prayer* (Orlando: Harcourt Brace, 1963, 1992), 91.

Part One

VALLEYS
of the
MIND

God Is
My Friend

*There are friends who
pretend to be friends,
but there is a friend who
sticks closer than a brother.*

— PROVERBS 18:24 RSV

1

LONELINESS

I am obscure to most of the world,
yet a tender eye guards my every step.
I sigh; an attentive ear listens;
I cry; a gentle hand brushes away the tears.

All the lonely people—where do they all come from?" asks the question from the popular Beatles' song. People from all walks of life, in all situations of life—in marriages, in families, in crowds, in the workplace, on the streets, in churches—these are the lonely people. Those who are alone may be lonely as well as those surrounded by multitudes.

Loneliness is a deep sadness of the heart. This heart does not yearn merely for a physical being but rather for another who freely offers true kindness and companionship. Loneliness is a separation, a separation of the heart from others. Quite often in this day and age of busyness, people are disconnected from one another, perhaps afraid to reveal any need for closeness. Whatever the reason, loneliness takes us to a valley of isolation, a valley of sadness.

In the book of Genesis we read of Leah, the surprise first wife of the patriarch Jacob. The elder of two sisters, given to Jacob in marriage through the deceit of her father, Laban, she began marriage, to say the least, in an awkward situation. Jacob had bargained for Rachel and had worked seven years to gain her. Laban, however, deceived Jacob and on his wedding night gave him Leah instead. It must have been devastating to watch her husband voice his disappointment the morning after taking her for his bride. What a terrible insult and hurt for a new bride! Jacob loved Rachel so much that he agreed to work another seven years for her. The honeymoon for Leah was short, for after only a week Rachel would become Jacob's second wife.

Though Leah was the first wife, she ranked far behind her younger sister Rachel in the eyes and heart of her husband, and she would spend many years trying to win Jacob's affections. Through all this, God took notice of her loneliness of heart and spirit. He saw that she was not loved and so He gave her children. Her firstborn was named Reuben because, she said, "It is because the LORD has seen my misery. Surely my husband will love me now" (Genesis 29:32). The Lord provided her with three more sons in succession, yet Jacob's love still belonged to Rachel.

At the birth of her fourth son she said, "This time I will praise the LORD." So she named him Judah (v. 35). The emptiness in Leah's heart was beginning to be filled with One who is all in all. She began to realize her joy must be dependent upon God, who never fails, rather than looking to those around her to meet her needs.

We don't often think of Leah as being blessed of God, but some interesting things about this woman stand out to me. Though unloved by her husband, she was not unloved by God, and He blessed her womb by making her fruitful.

She gave Jacob a total of six sons and one daughter whom she bore herself, plus two sons through her maidservant, Zilpah. Rachel, on the other hand, was barren for a long time. In that time and culture, sons were an important asset to a family, so Jacob had no choice but to include Leah in his life if he was to have sons.

In addition, Leah's third son, Levi, would become the head of the priestly lineage of Israel. She also gave birth to Judah, for whom she praised God (Genesis 29:35), from whom Israel's kings descended and from whose line came our Lord Jesus. And we learn that Jesus made His earthly dwelling in Nazareth in the land of Zebulun, Leah's sixth son. Leah would not know this about her sons, but God made her legacy sure.

As the large family of Jacob, along with his servants and cattle, traveled from the land of Paddan-aram back to Jacob's homeland, the love of his life, Rachel, died giving birth to her second son, Benjamin. She was buried near Bethlehem.

I'm sure Jacob felt a tremendous loneliness after Rachel died. The attachment he developed to his two youngest sons, her sons, would indicate he did. Yet I wonder if he ever had any thoughts of pity toward Leah and the loneliness she had experienced from his hand. I wonder if he sought consolation from his own loneliness in the companionship of the one who had so yearned for his love.

Unable to obtain Jacob's favor in life, Leah found in death a place of honor resting next to her husband. Sometime between the family's resettlement in Jacob's homeland

and their move to Egypt, Leah died. Jacob buried her in the tomb of his grandparents, Abraham and Sarah, where his parents, Isaac and Rebekah, were also buried and where he instructed his sons in Egypt to bury him also.

Leah, the unloved, the sad and lonely, the lowly, God faithfully exalted through the generations of her sons. And in her final resting place, she lay in the tomb of the "father of our faith." How like a gracious and good God to "keep track of all [our] sorrows" (Psalm 56:8 NLT).

Most of us have been touched by loneliness at one time or another, in one form or another. Most likely, we will never experience the extreme that Leah endured, but in whatever situation, the ache is much the same.

In *The Lion, the Witch and the Wardrobe,* C. S. Lewis describes the lonely night journey of Aslan the lion, who is a type of Christ, up the Hill of the Stone Table to offer himself as a sacrifice. He is suddenly aware that he is being followed and looks around to see his young friends Susan and Lucy. They beg him to allow them to walk with him. "'Well—' said Aslan and seemed to be thinking. Then he said, 'I should be glad of company tonight. Yes, you may come, if you will promise to stop when I tell you, and after that leave me to go on alone.'"

As they walk, Susan and Lucy notice how slowly and with a drooping head he goes. Aslan stumbles and, concerned, Susan asks him if he is ill. He replies:

> "No," said Aslan. "I am sad and lonely. Lay your hands on my mane so that I can feel you are there and let us walk like that."

And so the girls did what they would never have dared to do without his permission, but what they had longed to do ever since they first saw him—buried their cold hands in the beautiful sea of fur and stroked it and, so doing, walked with him.[1]

What a lovely and solemn picture of Christ as He endured the agony in the Garden of Gethsemane, in contemplation of the cross He would bear for the sins of people. He desired His closest companions, Peter, James, and John, near Him that sorrowful night, for He too was sad and lonely. We should be comforted by this, for He is able to sympathize with those who walk through the valley of loneliness. He was there for you and for me.

Loneliness is not a unique experience. All of us crave society with others. God created us for companionship. And He created us not only to need others but also to expend ourselves for the needs of those around us. Often the balm for our own cure is to reach out in love to someone else.

Father, it is painful when we feel no one cares.
Let those moments cultivate a deepening
intimacy with the Friend of sinners.
Remind us of Your precious promise that
we are never alone when we are Your children.

NOTE

1. C. S. Lewis, *The Lion, the Witch and the Wardrobe* (New York: Harper Trophy, 1950, 1994), 150.

God Is the Source
of All My
Righteousness

The people will declare, "The
Lord is the source of all my
righteousness and strength."

— ISAIAH 45:24 NLT

2

GUILT

*The soul was laid at Calvary's feet
and sin was dealt its fatal blow;
'twas covered by the Savior's blood
and washed as white as snow.*

In John Bunyan's great classic, *Pilgrim's Progress,* when the hero Christian was searching for a way to rid himself of the terrible burden of sin on his back, he was directed by Evangelist across a wide field to a wicket gate in the distance. As he entered through this gate to begin his famous journey on the straight and narrow path, he came to a highway fenced on both sides with a wall called Salvation. He attempted to run up the hill but was still weighed down by his burden. Upon reaching the top he found a cross, and as he approached the cross, his burden loosened of itself, dropped from his shoulders, and tumbled down the hill into the mouth of an open grave, where it was seen no more.

Like the pilgrim Christian, we have all carried our burden of sin and, like him, at the moment of our salvation, that burden was loosed forever. Little did we know the bondage we were under until the chains were broken. What a wonderful relief to be freed from sin, to know we are forgiven! Yet as we continue our journeys, some of us have a tendency to want to keep our "knapsack" of guilt. Though it is useful to bring us to repentance when we sin, guilt is a crippling enemy when we allow its tendrils to cling to us. We then become wrapped up in self rather than focusing on our God.

Most of us hold memories of bad choices and sins committed that carry heavy and lifelong consequences, times that we wish we could somehow alter. We need to remember that He has taken away our sins and the condemnation of the Law, nailing them to the cross (Colossians 2:14). When we continue to carry guilt that He has absolved, it is as if we said to Him, "It was not enough."

When you feel your past sins coming to the surface of your mind, it is a good practice to trace the lives of some of God's saints from the pages of His Word. The Bible paints candid pictures of these ordinary people, straightforward in its description of their successes and their failures.

By most standards, Rahab would not have been a likely candidate for the Bible's heroes of faith. She was born into the idolatrous nation of the Amorites, in the city of Jericho. The reputation of the Israelites and the God they served preceded them as they encamped across the Jordan River from Jericho. The nations heard how this God had brought the Israelites out of the land of Egypt and preserved them as they wandered in the wilderness.

Not only was Rahab an idolater, she was also a harlot, one of the city's prostitutes. Yet the second chapter of Joshua describes how she feared the God of Israel (verse 11) and how faith in this God was beginning to grow within her heart. She hid the two spies who had come to look over the land, and, confident that Israel would destroy Jericho as they had destroyed other cities, she made the spies promise that when war came they would protect her and her family. Because of Jericho's great wickedness, God had commanded Israel to destroy everything in the city.

The spies gave her their oath for protection and instructed her to hang a scarlet cord out of the window to identify her location within the city. In faith Rahab obeyed their command. Consequently, when the city of Jericho fell in defeat to the Israelites, Rahab and all who were with her were saved.

What a change in lifestyle Rahab and her family would make! It must have been intimidating to live among the Israelites at first. I have no doubt that she felt her shame and guilt, aware that people probably knew what her occupation had been. The eyes of the Israelite women must have looked upon her with curiosity, if not a little contempt. Yet I believe Rahab, by this time, had fully accepted this awesome God of the Hebrews. She had seen Him accomplish the destruction of Jericho and all its inhabitants. She had risked her life to save the spies, and God would remember.

I find it fascinating that the only person in the whole city of Jericho who had a reverent fear of the almighty God was one of its most infamous citizens. The stories that preceded the invasion of the Israelites had certainly created fear among the city's occupants, but this woman had been given the essential fear that instilled the truth of Jehovah in her heart. She believed God was who He said

He was when she told the spies, "For the LORD your God is God in heaven above and on the earth below" (Joshua 2:11). She acted accordingly. This harlot had no inhibitions about asking the spies to show kindness to her family, for she also had come to understand His mercy.

This is not the last time we hear of Rahab in the Bible. She later married one of the men of the tribe of Judah. Is it not remarkable that our God elevates the lowest of people, the outcast, the unclean? When clothed in the righteousness of the Lord, the most defiled becomes pure. So the story of Rahab is perpetuated for generations, for she became the mother of Boaz, who married Ruth, the grandmother of Jesse, the father of King David.

The genealogy, of course, traces down to the Lord Jesus Himself. Rahab is listed along with Tamar and Ruth, the only three women named (Bathsheba is called the wife of Uriah the Hittite) in the genealogical tree of Christ recorded in the book of Matthew. All of these women were Gentiles. The Bible makes so clear that Christ came to save sinners, and He has chosen those whom most of us would find appalling to become the heroes in the hall of faith. You find these unlikely heroes abounding in Scripture, some of them very much like you and I.

God takes even the worst parts of our lives and uses them for His glory. Bury your guilt beneath the blood of the Cross, and use your past experiences as a tool to help others, not as a crutch to make you an invalid in His kingdom and hinder you in the race. Don't let Satan rob you of the great opportunity to honor your Lord.

GUILT

~

Father, thank You for the righteousness of Christ
who takes away the sins of the world.
Help us to rejoice that **all** *our sins are forgiven*
because He has nailed them to the Cross.

The Lord Is My Shepherd

The Lord is my shepherd; I shall not want.
He makes me to lie down in green pastures;
He leads me beside the still waters.

Yea, though I walk through the
valley of the shadow of death,
I will fear no evil; for You are with me;
Your rod and Your staff, they comfort me.

PSALM 23:1–2, 4 NKJV

3

FEAR

Fear is a powerful emotion. It can cripple and paralyze a person into helplessness, or it can incite one to great feats of courage. Fear can be a good emotion, for it can create caution and alertness; it can also be adverse, for it can produce anxiety and worry. Each of us has known fear of one kind or another.

God has given us a built-in "radar" for danger, which is a healthy fear. This signal prompts us into appropriate action to respond to dangers or challenges. But millions of people are immobilized by certain stimuli that produce a paranoia type of fear, or phobia. The most common psychiatric conditions in the United States are anxiety disorders. We are told that about 25 million Americans experience anxiety disorders at some time during their lives.

About 330 years before the birth of Christ, during the reign of the Persian Empire, many Jews living throughout the provinces of the empire had returned to their homeland after their seventy-year captivity by the Babylonians had ended. Many other Jews chose to remain in various parts of the empire. There lived at this time in the capital city of Susa a beautiful young Jewess by the name of Hadassah. Hadassah, also called Esther, was an orphan and was raised as a daughter by a close relative named Mordecai, who was a loyal palace official.

King Xerxes, the ruler over this empire, gave a grand festival for his princes and officials. His beautiful queen, Vashti, refused the king's command to present herself before his court of people and nobles. Infuriated at her disobedience, the king deposed Queen Vashti. At the proposal of his personal attendants, Xerxes began a search for a new queen and had beautiful girls from every province brought into his harem at Susa. From these virgins he would select a new queen.

Esther was among the maidens chosen for the harem. She kept her nationality a secret because Mordecai had given her instructions to do so. Because of his affection and care, Mordecai inquired daily at the court as to Esther's welfare, and she continued to be obedient to his counsel as she had always been.

As so often is the case, God worked in the hearts of those surrounding His people to enable them to accomplish His purposes. During the time of her preparation before being presented to the king, Esther found favor in the eyes of the harem's keeper. Eventually she also found the king's favor, and he crowned her his new queen.

Enter the villain of the story and the enemy of God— an evil, high-ranking official of the king's court named Haman. Haman hated the Jews, Mordecai in particular, because as a Jew Mordecai refused to bow down to him as others did when Haman passed through the city streets. Haman began to seek a way to destroy Mordecai and the Jewish population in all the provinces of Persia.

Haman presented a plan to the king to destroy this people within the land, because "their laws are different from those of every other people, and they do not keep the king's laws, so that it is not for the king's profit to tolerate them" (Esther 3:8 RSV). The king accommodated Haman by issuing a decree that the Jews be destroyed, sealing the edict with his signet ring.

A great fear and mourning came over the Jews in all the provinces of the land. Mordecai dressed in sackcloth and mourned loudly in the city. Not knowing the reason for his behavior, Esther was deeply troubled and ordered an attendant to find out what was the matter with Mordecai. Mordecai in turn told the attendant about the edict set in place at the order of Haman. He appealed to Queen Esther to approach the king and beg for mercy for her people.

It is important for us to understand that it was certain death for any person, even the queen, to approach the king's inner court unless the person had been summoned. This young woman, taken from the love and security of her home, in the harem of a pagan king, surely experienced a great deal of anxiety and fear. Then upon learning the dilemma of her people, what terror and grief must have seized her emotions. She had been chosen queen, yet she was still subject to the laws and decrees of the land.

Mordecai's warning to Esther was that she also would be included in the annihilation of the Jews if the decree were effected. He told her if she kept silent, deliverance for the Jews would come from another source. Yet he encouraged Esther by suggesting that she may have been placed in her royal position by divine providence "for such a time as this." Esther instructed Mordecai to fast and presumably also to pray, and she and her maids would do the same. Then Esther would go to the king "and if I perish, I perish" (Esther 4:16).

The Bible tells us the fear of the Lord is the beginning of wisdom. Our fear of God is based on how we perceive Him—the great Creator of all things, who sustains and controls His creation, the holy and righteous God Almighty who is full of grace and mercy, yet exercises His wrath in righteousness. He is our Father, and with reverence and awe we worship Him in spirit and truth, and with trembling.

Esther had been raised in the nurture of this God and, although His name is not mentioned in the book of Esther, His presence is evidenced by the working out of His plan for His chosen people in the midst of the enemy.

Esther dared to approach the king. When he saw her, "she found favor in his sight and he held out to Esther the golden scepter that was in his hand. Then Esther approached and touched the top of the scepter" (Esther 5:2–3 RSV). The king asked what was her request.

Esther devised a plan whereby she entertained the king and Haman, who pompously prided himself that the queen would invite him to her banquet. Then she held a second banquet, again inviting Haman. At this banquet Esther revealed herself and her people to the king, pleading for their lives. Outraged, Xerxes demanded to know who it was who had planned to exterminate the Jewish people, and Esther disclosed the evil plans of Haman.

Haman suffered the death on the gallows that he had planned for Mordecai, and the Jews were saved from destruction by the courageous act of a queen who defied all odds because she feared her God more than she feared man.

Each time I read the verses of the king's outstretched scepter, they warm my heart. I always think of approaching the throne of God where, because of my Jesus, I find favor in His sight, and His scepter is always held out to me in love. I can draw near to His throne because I am always accepted in the beloved Christ.

Our fear of the living God is our means of overcoming the unnecessary fears of this life. When they saw the manifestation of God's power after the reading of the Ten Commandments, Moses told the Israelites, "Do not be afraid. God has come to test you, so that the fear of God will be with you to keep you from sinning" (Exodus 20:20). Sinning against this holy God was the only thing they needed to fear. This fear of God helps us make right choices.

Life is fragile and full of uncertainties. There is plenty in this world to make us fear. Believers, however, need not fear as others fear; we are told to "cast our cares upon the Lord." The difference is explained by Jesus in chapter 12 of Luke's gospel when He tells us, "Do not be afraid of those who kill the body and after that can do no more. But I will show you whom you should fear: Fear him who, after the killing of the body, has power to throw you into hell" (verses 4–5). Then in verse 7, He assures His children that "the very hairs of your head are all numbered." And further in verse 32, He comforts us, "Do not be afraid, little flock, for your Father has been pleased to give you the kingdom." These assurances give us the courage to face life's uncertainties with certainty—that our strength lies not within our power but in Him.

Father, give us the wisdom to
fear You with a holy fear,
that we may face each day
with the assurance that
all of our steps are guided by You.

God Is
My Place
of Safety

You are my strength;
I wait for you to rescue me,
for you, O God,
are my place of safety.

PSALM 59:9 NLT

4

REJECTION

Our valleys nestle within
different mountain confines,
but the Guardian of our souls always
answers to the echo of our voices,
no matter how remote each may be.

As you read through the Gospel accounts of the ministry of Jesus as He traveled this earth, a simple image emerges: His acceptance by the outcasts of society and His rejection by the elite religious sects of Israel. He was sent to the lost sheep of the house of Israel, yet the religious leaders, the ones who should have known who He was, were the very ones who hated Him the most. Jesus came to "seek and save that which was lost," and His ministry reached and touched the hearts of the most undignified and looked-down-upon people in the regions where He walked.

The simple and profound parables and stories that Jesus related to the crowds spoke to the depth of where the common man and woman lived—their depth of pain, depravity, and hopelessness. The Lord did not offer a physical escape from the pains of life. Rather He showed them a path that would give them hope and subsequent joy to journey through the valley.

One thing that can weight the heart with despair is feeling rejected and unloved. Vast numbers of people awaken to each new day with this heavy burden. As they seek to find their place in a cruel and unfriendly world, they encounter isolation and loneliness.

Jesus encountered such a woman. She was a Canaanite from the idolatrous region of Tyre and Sidon, despised by the Jewish population and commonly referred to by the Jews as "dogs."

This woman also suffered from another pain that superseded her concern for acceptability to society. She was the mother of a daughter who was demon possessed. The woman had no lack of determination to entreat the Lord for mercy and healing for her child. She put aside any sign of pride to have an audience with the Great Physician, whose reputation had so spread that He seldom found refuge from the crowds.

As evidenced throughout the Gospels, Jesus' compassion for the multitudes who were like "sheep without a shepherd" exceeded His concern for His personal needs.

A surprising part of this story, however, is that the Lord Himself seemed to reject this poor woman. As a matter of fact, it appeared at first that, by His silence, He completely ignored her when she fell at His feet and begged Him to cast the demon out of her daughter. As she persisted in her plea, the Lord's remarks could have put the woman off entirely as He seemingly reproached her when He told her, "It isn't right to take food from the children [of Israel] and throw it to the dogs [the Gentiles]" (Matthew 15:26 NLT).

We are reminded of the incident in Genesis 32 when Jacob wrestled all night with the Angel of the Lord and refused to let Him go unless He blessed him. The Lord did indeed bless Jacob. This woman also held on for her blessing.

This mother, with true resolve, replied to Jesus, "Yes, Lord, but even dogs are permitted to eat crumbs that fall beneath their master's table" (Matthew 15:27 NLT). As a result of her faith, the Lord healed her daughter.

The disciples learned a great lesson that day. They had told the Lord to send her away—even they were filled with the prideful thought that this "outsider" could not approach the Lord. Her faith was tested and strengthened, and the disciples discovered that those rejected by the chosen nation of Israel were also included as part of Christ's sheep. The Lord will never reject anyone who comes to Him in true faith as his only hope.

So many face great obstacles in life because of the heartache of rejection they have experienced. Growing up in a home and family where they were never confirmed and nurtured to grow into confident adults, they stumble through situations and relationships with doubts and uncertainty.

A very close friend of mine (we'll call her Nancy) grew up in a home where her parents were never pleased with anything she did. Even as a small child, it seemed she could never do anything right. Nancy was smart, an honor student. She participated in a lot of school activities and worked hard at home, yet all she ever received were complaints and criticism. Her father seldom spoke to her except to belittle whatever happened to be important to her.

Nancy struggled with her problems of rejection. She felt she could never measure up to any accomplishment or expectation. Nancy was afraid to trust others because when anyone complimented her, she couldn't believe the person was serious. She suffered tremendously under the burden of insecurity and failure. Even when she married, she never really thought of herself as a capable wife or mother.

Then Nancy came to a crossroad in her life, and there she met One who accepted her just as she was—imperfect but made whole through His sacrifice. He helped her to begin to see her worth was in Him. The Savior took her rejection upon Himself, and she no longer had to carry it. She would continue to face challenges on occasion, yet she no longer felt unloved and unlovely. Her heart was healing.

An old fable by Hans Christian Andersen called *The Ugly Duckling* describes a perfect example of what many people go through. Probably most people will recognize the story of this forlorn little bird born among ducklings. His mother and brothers and sisters called him ugly, and all the barnyard birds pushed and pecked at him. No one was kind. Because all those around him thought him ugly, no one accepted him.

The little guy was forced to leave home and family and wander alone. Even the wild ducks refused to have anything to do with him. He happened upon a cottage of an old woman and her cat and chicken, where he sought to find a home. They too looked down on him, and out into the world he again trudged.

Finally he came to a lake where he could at least swim

and dive. He noticed some beautiful birds flying overhead although, at that time, he didn't know they were swans. He only knew they had each other and he was sad and lonely. The poor duckling spent the long, cold winter in the marshes alone in misery.

When spring came and the sun was again warm, he spread his wings and flew away to another lake. Spotting a group of the beautiful birds that he had seen before winter came, he decided to take a chance and join them—even at the risk of being pecked and scorned because of his ugliness. As he glided over the lake and looked down into the water, he suddenly caught sight of his reflection, no longer the ugly duckling but a lovely, long-necked swan, just like the rest of the beautiful birds around him. The pain and misery he had endured would be forgotten because he finally found where he belonged.

The little ugly duckling came to realize his true beauty when he saw that his reflection in the lake matched that of the lovely swans around him. When we as children of God realize where we truly belong and to whom, we are able to understand our true beauty and worth. Jesus was despised and rejected of men, and though we may endure that sorrow also, may we be reflections of His image to others.

*Father, how precious in
Your sight is each of Your children.
So precious that Your only Son laid down
His life for us. He has made us
worthy before You by His blood.*

The Lord
Is My
Victory

*Stand still, and see
the victory of the Lord
on your behalf.*

— 2 CHRONICLES 20:17 RSV

5

FAILURE

*He feeds us still and then increases
the basketfuls of broken pieces.*

"If at first you don't succeed, try, try again." That's some good advice that most of us were taught from our early years. If you think of the many people who have made significant contributions to our world, you will realize that none of them succeeded without having failed, at least once, in their endeavors.

Everyone can relate to failure. In one form or another all of us have experienced the humiliation and, sometimes, devastation of failure. The road of life we travel includes a lot of unknown curves and detours. As we view our life's map, just as we view an ordinary road map, the inconvenient or restricted spots are not always visible, nor are we always made aware of road construction or trouble areas such as landslides or washed-out roads. These unexpected difficulties usually come as a surprise and aggravation to most of us. Failure defeats some and energizes others.

Failure may also be characterized by one's definition of the word. The world is often puzzled by the tirelessness of

Christians whose quests seem insignificant. These Christians face tremendous odds with seemingly little success. Yet they continue, undaunted by their setbacks. The world is often quick to label the small things of God as insignificant and trivial, truly failures in its sight. But God takes the small things and the failures, even the foolish failures, of His people and amazes the "wise" of this world with His blessings.

One such remarkable Christian who appeared defeated even before she got started was Gladys Aylward, the little woman from England who yearned to go and give the Gospel of Jesus Christ to the people of China who had never heard this Good News. No missionary society wanted her. They thought her education was too limited, and they determined the language was too difficult for her to learn.

Gladys was unthwarted. God had placed this desire in her heart, and she would find a way to go. During those frustrating times when all those around her discouraged her plans, she learned to pray with fervor. God brought people into her life who showed her what true faith really meant. Her hunger to know God's Word began to increase. She gained courage from reading about Abraham and Moses, who left the security of their homes to obey the call of God. And when reading the details of Nehemiah's story, she determined this God who called him to return to Jerusalem was the same God who was calling her to go to China.

God arranged for her journey, step-by-step, and slowly Gladys arrived at the day of her departure for China. In

October of 1932, she left with few possessions and little money, and alone. Her venture would take her through many long days of travel and harrowing experiences, enduring the cold of Russia and the theft of the few belongings she had brought with her. Yet with each setback, Gladys remembered her calling and faithfully trudged forward. Finally, twenty-six days later, her tired feet touched the soil of China.

The little missionary would go through many hardships during her period in this land she grew to love. Gladys came to be known as the "storyteller," for she told the Good News of Christ through Bible stories. She labored among the outcasts of the land—the poor, the afflicted, and the helpless. She became one of them in dress, in speech, and even in thought. Children especially loved her. No obstacle was too difficult to tackle for the God she loved and worshiped. He never failed her, and the miracles He accomplished through this ordinary woman were astonishing.

Another woman of almost obscure description is introduced to us in 2 Kings, chapter 5. Only two verses, 2 and 3, mention her—and we don't even know her name. Yet great was the impact this maiden had upon her master.

This unnamed child was taken captive by the army of Naaman, a great commander of the armies of the king of Aram. She was given as a handmaid to his wife. Though valiant in service to his king and highly regarded, Naaman suffered from the shameful disease of leprosy.

It is hard for us to imagine what horror and pain it would have been to be taken away from everything and everyone we hold dear in life. To be young and vulnerable and to be subjected to a pagan culture would be calamitous. I can conceive of this young girl lying in bed at night, wondering what happened to her family. Would she ever see them again? Yet we sense no bitterness as she attended to her duties to her mistress. Apparently, from our brief text, she not only claimed Israel as her birthright, but she also claimed the God of Israel in her heart. She therefore knew God was with her, even in a foreign land.

Learning of her master's disease, and probably having gained favor in Naaman's household by this time, she faithfully told her mistress of her God's power by telling her, "If only my master would see the prophet who is in Samaria! He would cure him of his leprosy" (2 Kings 5:3). Her mistress relayed the message to her husband. Perhaps they had some knowledge of this God and of the great prophet Elisha also, or perhaps they were desperate enough to try anything.

Naaman's action was swift to find the prophet, and he received permission from his king to do so. Consequently, we learn later in the chapter, he was indeed healed. Naaman had taken many gifts to Elisha for this cure, none of which the prophet accepted. We can imagine, however, his return home to his wife and the little maiden who had guided him to the place of healing. I think he might have rewarded the little girl greatly. We can hope he found healing not only for his body but for his soul.

Our greatest poverty is often the greatest gift we can offer to the Master.

Gladys Aylward freely relinquished all she possessed in

this life to share her gift of faith with prisoners of darkness. This nameless maiden, void of possessions, family, and freedom, gave God her faithfulness in the midst of her valley and thereby brought great gifts to the prisoners of the house of Naaman.

All the barriers and setbacks we face are allowed by the design of God's providence. He takes our failures and uses them to perfect our walk with Him, to teach us the valuable lesson of keeping our focus heavenward as we travel the narrow road.

As children of God, we must use our failures as a means of trusting Him more. The Lord intends those situations to draw us to a deeper dependence on Him, being confident that even our greatest mistakes can be turned around for His glory.

Perhaps you have failed in your marriage or as a parent, in your job, or as a friend. Your failures may be self-inflicted, or they may be beyond your control. Whatever your circumstance, look to God in the midst of your failure, dear friend, and don't lose heart. You'll find yourself in the company of all God's travelers on this road of life.

Father, help us to realize we are nothing without You. Even in life's failures and disappointments, let us see Your grace working in our lives, and that Your strength is shown when we are weak. Motivate our hearts to honor You in all circumstances.

God Is
My Refuge

*The eternal God is thy refuge,
and underneath are the everlasting arms.*

~ DEUTERONOMY 33:27 KJV

6

INSECURITY

Every burden released to God
is as a dried twig broken from the heart
to allow room for new growth.

$\mathcal{I}$ never understood where her father was, because I was always told that I was too young to understand. Perhaps. But I still wondered. As I grew older, I began to comprehend why I was never told. Things of that nature were not discussed in families at that time. It was a shameful subject.

I always thought her to be very fortunate, since she lived with my gramma and grandpa, along with her mother and unmarried uncles. Growing up, I adored her and looked forward to the times our family visited her house. To me she was beautiful and sweet, and I remember her treating me special, never considering me a pest, even though I'm sure at times I was. She was older than I and seemed more like a sister than a cousin. When she married, my child's heart suffered for my loss tremendously—though later I came to realize what a wonderful man her husband was.

It would be several years more before I figured out why she did not have a father, and it would be many years after that before I comprehended the terrible effect growing up without that important person had on her.

At a time when a young woman bearing a child out of wedlock was a disgraceful and humiliating incident in a family, regardless of whether the pregnancy resulted from a consensual relationship or from rape, Frances faced many obstacles as a child. Because of her mother's indiscretion, she suffered the injustice of scorn and gossip from cruel and insensitive people. She called Grandpa her "daddy" because there was no one else to bear that title in her small world. At school, her classmates didn't know the truth, so for the most part she escaped the alienation of her friends.

She realized at a very early age that her father was missing but, out of fear, never asked about him. It was a difficult and confusing period for her. The worst part was the secret that was kept from her within her family. Who was her father? Why did he leave her? Why did he not love her? The anguish and bewilderment of a child without an explanation caused much anxiety and guilt within her. She remembered conversations between her mother and uncles, with remarks about "keeping an eye on Frances," because her father might kidnap her. That is how she discovered his identity. They intended never to let her father near her. In the meantime, she learned she had an older half-brother, and she often wondered if he knew about her.

Once, in an earlier time, an unusual drama was unfolding in 1 Kings 17. Elijah was a great prophet of God in the kingdom of Israel during the reign of wicked King Ahab and his even more wicked wife, Jezebel. The prophet decreed a coming drought in the land, unceasing until he spoke the word for it to end. The dramatic story includes the prophet's flight to the wilderness to the Brook of Cherith, where God gave him drink and would give him food delivered by ravens; and then the drying up of the brook, at which time God instructed him to go for provisions to an alien land to the home of a Gentile widow and her son, who were dying from the famine.

Being a widow under normal circumstances was hard enough during this period in history. This poor woman was apparently devoid of any friends or relations who might help her in her pitiful state. It would be difficult to imagine the helplessness of this widow, weak and vulnerable not only physically but emotionally. The concern of a mother for her son would be to protect him at all costs. Yet she had no one to whom she could turn. They now awaited death.

The drought was so severe that she was preparing her final meal for herself and her son when the prophet Elijah approached her. There was no hesitation to bring him some water when he asked her, but at the request for a morsel of food, she explained her destitution and inability to feed him. It is obvious from her remarks that she knew about the God of Israel, Elijah's God, and sensed that Elijah was more than just an ordinary beggar. She therefore obeyed him when he told her to fix him a small cake from the last of the flour and oil that she possessed. He prefaced his request by telling her not to fear. Then he assured her that God would not let her flour be used up nor allow her oil to run dry "until the day the Lord sends rain on the earth" (1 Kings 17:14 NKJV).

This dear woman, whose name is not recorded, whose future was anything but secure, was sustained by the God who would use her to provide for His prophet.

God takes the poverty of our lives to exhibit the riches of His grace for others and for ourselves. God provided for the little household as Elijah's visit was prolonged for about three years. During this time the widow must have grown in her faith under the teaching of Elijah, and she must have become very content and secure. The drought continued all around her, yet never did she or her son hunger.

Her predicament was not yet over, however, for after some time the son she feared would die of starvation took ill and died of the disease. Devastated and fearing that sin within her was the cause, she thought God had sent Elijah to punish her. God again strengthened her faith by raising her son from the dead through the prophet.

It was probably a sad time for the widow when Elijah was called to leave her and her son. I believe it was sad for Elijah also. Yet I think by this stage of her life, she no longer felt alone and insecure. She had witnessed the remarkable faithfulness of the Lord God and His servant Elijah, and, though perhaps sad, she was thankful at having been chosen for this special bestowal of grace. I like to think this was not the last time Elijah visited the widow but that there were occasions when they met again.

This nameless widow, poor and alone, was also singled out by our Lord Jesus when He referred to the many widows "in Israel in the days of Elijah, when the heaven was shut up three years and six months, and there was a great famine throughout all the land; but to none of them was Elijah sent except to Zarephath, in the region of Sidon, to a woman who was a widow" (Luke 4:25–26 NKJV)—another blessed remembrance of an insignificant Gentile.

To this day, my cousin Frances has never known the entire truth about her missing parent. Her mother still will not discuss many of the details. Frances's father died while she was still a teenager. Years later, after she had many bouts with depression and anger, the Lord came into her life and slowly began to heal some of the deep wounds she carried. Just as the Lord touched the poor widow of Zarephath, so He touched my cousin.

She finally met her brother, and he gave her some information about their dad's life. Her father did want to be involved in her life but was not allowed to by her family. Her brother had also wanted to know her but could not under the circumstances. The weight of the unknown began to gradually lift from Frances's shoulders.

As in the case of the widow, my cousin Frances had never known the security of a father in this life, but she came to rest in a Father who would be with her forever. A Father in whom she could put all her confidence and know fully and completely that His love for her will never change. Though her childhood was riddled with fear and sadness, she can now rest in the assurance that this Father has watched over her in her darkest hours and that He will never leave nor forsake her. She can now rest in the security of a heavenly Father forever.

Father, what comfort we find in knowing that
in You we are secure eternally.
Though life riddles us with sadness and pain,
we rest in the assurance of
Your constant companionship.

God Is
the Source of
All My Joy

*There I will go to
the altar of God, to God—
the source of all my joy.*

~ PSALM 43:4 NLT

7

GROWING OLD

So, teach us, O Lord, to number our days,
for we are as sand on the shore,
to live with fullness the life You've given,
till time shall be no more
and eternity is all.

I love the autumn of the year. The changing colors of the trees, the smells, the crispness of the air, the final harvest of the year. The fall season also inevitably brings a certain melancholy for me because it ushers in shorter days and the approaching of another year gone by. Such are the seasons of our lives—the autumn years remind us of the brevity of our days on this earth. If God allows us to live, each of us will grow old. But how we grow old is sometimes a matter of choice.

Gert wore a continual smile on her face and always had a kind word for everyone. This was quite amazing because one would not have thought she had a lot to smile about. This lady had been widowed for many years. She had suffered a stroke, which limited her activities considerably; though she still lived on her own, she depended for the most part on others to care for her. She relied on a walker to move about. Her speech was impaired, yet she never complained. To be in her presence was to be in the presence of true joy.

I'm sure all of us have been in the company of a person who so exemplifies Christ that we feel somehow discomfited in the person's presence. Gert's granddaughter became my daughter-in-law. I remember the first time I met Gert I was impressed by her kindness and warmth. She always gave a vigorous hug and always that wonderful smile. She adored her family and thoroughly enjoyed life in spite of her limitations. At our son and daughter-in-law's wedding, she relished every moment of their happiness, remaining at the reception until all the other guests had departed. What a rare jewel to find in such a self-centered world!

Gert went to be with her Lord a few years ago. At her funeral, the tributes of her pastor and family and friends were poignant reminders of just how sweet her life had been to others. She had learned the secret to contentment regardless of circumstances. Her joyful disposition was a beautiful reflection of a soul at rest in God. Though her world may not have encompassed a great many people, those who did encounter her were deeply affected and knew she possessed an invaluable gift of inner joy. One of her grandchildren wrote, "Your radiant grin amidst a life filled with pain, we'll never know how much you kept from us, but we do know how much we all gained."

This was a woman whose life graced those around her. Despite Gert's frailty, she grew old gracefully and beautifully in the Lord.

Growing old is a fact of life, one which most of us

don't look forward to. The moment we are born, we begin on this journey. As our bodies begin to slow down, the eyes grow dim, and the senses dull, we are reminded of the solemn fact that our lives here on earth are but "a vapor that appears for a little time and then vanishes away" (James 4:14 NKJV).

For the believer, growing old can be a time of great usefulness to our Master and fulfillment. Wisdom gained through experiences along life's path can serve as loving instruction to those with whom we have contact. A cheerful countenance, like Gert's, can act as a magnet to those who need encouragement, because it reflects a cheerful heart. God orchestrates our circumstances, whether in good health or ill; He has determined the number of our days on this earth. The heart that has cultivated an abiding relationship with Him will begin to reflect on His wonderful faithfulness in days gone by, knowing His strength will be sufficient through days of suffering and uncertainty.

The most precious and fragrant spices and ointments are derived from plants by various means. The prized oils are extracted through the process of cutting the bark from the trees or, as in the case of olive oil, the crushing of the fruit of the tree. Many of these spices and oils were required in the sacrifices of the Jews and in the ministrations of the priests in the tabernacle. The Bible calls them "a memorial on the altar . . . a sweet aroma to the Lord."

In the same manner, His people are "peeled and crushed" in order to produce that same pleasing fragrance to the Lord. The apostle Paul likens the Christian life to spreading the "fragrance of the knowledge of [Christ]."

Our Father intends us to be that sweet aroma to those around us regardless of our situation. And we know, in Him, that is possible. An aged person, though perhaps frail and ill, can still permeate the lives of others with that fragrance.

I often think of Gert, and I know she left deep impressions on those who were acquainted with her. I'm sure she did not have the slightest idea that the fragrance of her life touched so many in such special ways. It was simply an outpouring of what lay in her heart. I pray that, if God permits, I may grow old, as she did, with the grace of joy in spite of what my circumstances may be.

Father, we know as our
outer bodies may weaken,
our inner spirits may grow stronger
in the power of Your strength.
Help us to spread the
fragrance of Christ to others
that their lives may be refreshed
by Your presence in us.

Part Two

VALLEYS
of the
SPIRIT

The Lord
Is My Cup
of Blessing

Lord, you alone are my inheritance,
my cup of blessing.
You guard all that is mine.

PSALM 16:5 NLT

8

WHEN DREAMS
ARE SHATTERED

*Let God be the hope of your life,
and your dreams will never disappoint you.*

There was nothing exceptional in Silas Marner—he was an ordinary weaver, engaged to be married, a young man in good standing with the church, and fortunate to have a friend he considered as close as a brother. Although he was seen as a little odd, he was hardworking and honest and diligent in his duties as a citizen and a Christian. All things pointed forward to a happy, contented life.

One of the elder deacons of the church fell ill and, since he was without wife or children, had to be tended by the congregation. During Silas's turn to care for the deacon, the deacon died. A bag of money was discovered missing, and Silas's knife was found in the money drawer. As a search of Silas's room was conducted, his best friend, William, uncovered the empty money bag. Silas then remembered the last time he used his knife was to help William cut a strap of leather, but he remained silent to the others about this.

Silas maintained his innocence and was brought before

the church for the drawing of lots to convict or exonerate him. The lots pointed to his guilt. Crushed by the betrayal of his friend and now, he felt, by God Himself, Silas predicted his fiancée would also desert him. She did and within a month had married his best friend.

Silas moved to a distant village, isolating himself from all people and, he thought, from God also. Naturally the townspeople thought him strange and creepy, and all kinds of rumors surfaced regarding him. Silas, however, immersed himself in his work of weaving, and the cloth he produced now began to bring in a good sum of money. He labored even harder, hoarding his earnings, and soon had quite a stash of gold. This gold, hidden beneath the bricks on his hearth, became his companion. His only enjoyment, more an obsession, was counting his coins each day.

One dark and foggy night, the weaver's home was robbed. Devastated and enraged, he set out for the village, determined to find the thief. Some of the men were gathered at a local tavern, and Silas burst in among them with the lament of his loss. Since his gold had been one of the main separations between himself and the people of the town, the disaster of losing that gold seemed to be the catalyst that would begin to bridge the separation. With the help of the local people, Silas began to reenter the community of man that he had spurned so many years before.

Time passed with no word of the thief having been apprehended. As Silas sulked and dreamed of his lost idol one New Year's Eve, he missed the intrusion of a small girl who wandered into his cottage through the open cottage door. Upon awaking from his reverie, he noticed a bundle of gold shining before the fire and, because of his bad eye-sight, thought his gold had been returned. As he examined the hearth closer, he found that his "gold" was the hair of the tiny girl.

Silas realized this lass must have a mother, and he be-gan searching outside his cottage for her. He came upon the poor woman, overdosed with opium and quite dead. The villagers tried to get Silas to give the child up to a family who could care for her, but he refused. He indeed had recovered a much more valuable bag of gold in this lit-tle girl, whose name was Eppie, and he was not about to part with her.

Though Silas sought to prove his innocence in the crime he had been falsely accused of in the village of his youth, this mystery would remain with him for the rest of his life. He was content, however, because the pieces of his life that had been so crushed by disappointing circum-stances were mended when Eppie entered his existence and heart. She would bring Silas back from a life of shattered dreams and point his heart to joy he had never imagined.

Because we are mortal and vulnerable, sometimes life just doesn't work out the way we would like. Disappoint-ments come daily from many avenues. Some things touch us with reality perhaps after years of hope, then denial, un-til finally the pain of acceptance is settled. We accept that we will probably remain single. That we won't be able to have children. That we will not achieve the career goal set so long ago. Or we struggle with a shattered self-image be-cause of the consequences of foolish choices. The betrayal of a friend or family member. A failed marriage. Sudden illness or death. The list is long and can create feelings of helplessness or remorse.

In his book *Living with Your Dreams,* author David A. Seamands calls these times "our dark dungeon of disappointment." As our heavenly Father so often does, He means our disappointments to bring our priorities into proper focus. Someone has said those *disappointments* are *His appointments.* God's plans for our lives are not always what we envision they should be, but His plans are always for our good.

There was another pair of friends hundreds of years ago—one the son of a king, the other a future king himself. These friends were different from our story of Silas Marner, however, because they were both pledged to each other in the bond of love. The king's son knew his beloved friend was God's chosen king for Israel and pledged his lifelong loyalty to him, yielding to him his robe and armor as well as his sword as a token of his allegiance.

King Saul himself knew God had chosen David to replace him, yet in his hatred and bitterness he tried to kill David. Saul's son Jonathan was devastated by his father's malice toward David. For years David was pursued by this madman, though he had done nothing to merit Saul's hatred.

David had been anointed king by the prophet Samuel and was destined for the throne. Yet even though Saul wanted him dead, David was so dedicated to the present king that he would not dare harm him even when he had the opportunity to do so. David's heart was broken, for he knew the ties between him and his dear friend would be forever severed because of the hatred and disobedience of Saul. In their final meeting both young men wept as they parted for the last time, again pledging their friendship to each other. Saul and his son Jonathan were eventually killed in the midst of battle.

The dark valley of broken dreams. We all have them. In Christ, however, we all can have renewed dreams. The disciples saw their visions crumble when the Lord hung dying on the cross. How could they ever have foreseen the remarkable victory from such a shameful ending? Later this small band of fearful people would ignite the world with the good news of the Resurrection. Even the tomb could not extinguish the promises that Christ brought. Death could not hold Him. And I would proclaim neither can death withhold from His children the eternal hope that He has given us.

I love happy endings to stories. George Eliot's novel *Silas Marner* ends with the true joy of life given to Silas by the little golden-haired girl who invaded his shattered and embittered heart. The wonderful news for the child of Jesus Christ is that our ending only opens the door to our eternal beginning. "For our light and momentary troubles are achieving for us an eternal glory that far outweighs them all. So we fix our eyes not on what is seen, but on what is unseen. For what is seen is temporary, but what is unseen is eternal" (2 Corinthians 4:17–18).

Lord, as Your children,
help us to accept the disappointments in our
lives as Your intervening love for our good.
Give us encouragement as we remember
You are working out Your purposes for us.

God Is
My Wide River
of Protection

The Lord will be our Mighty One.
He will be like a wide river of
protection that no enemy can cross.

ISAIAH 33:21 NLT

9

INJUSTICE

*It is difficult to make a man
miserable while he feels he is worthy
of himself and claims kindred
to the great God who made him.*
(ABRAHAM LINCOLN)

Shoot all the bluejays you want, if you can hit 'em,
but remember it's a sin to kill a mockingbird." So said
Atticus Finch to his son, Jem, after giving him an air rifle.
Their neighbor told Jem why a person should never shoot
a mockingbird: "Mockingbirds don't do one thing but
make music for us to enjoy . . . they don't do one thing but
sing their hearts out for us."[1]

One of my favorite books, *To Kill a Mockingbird,* depicts the saga of the Finch family who lived in Alabama
during the mid-1930s, at a time in our nation's history
when segregation was still a strong presence, especially in
the South. It is a story of young Jem and his sister, Scout,
who learned, in the deepest sense, the ever-present reality
of the unfairness of life. On the other hand, they also
learned the meaning of honor and integrity, of courage
coupled with compassion for others in the face of all
odds—traits that are shown in the person of their father,
Atticus Finch. His philosophy of life was echoed in his

words to Scout as he was trying to help her adjust to her first year of school. "First of all," he said, "if you can learn a simple trick, Scout, you'll get along a lot better with all kinds of folks. You never really understand a person until you consider things from his point of view—until you climb into his skin and walk around in it."[2]

During one particular summer, Jem and Scout learned a great lesson about "climbing into another person's skin." The lesson would expose the children to the inequities of evil individuals against innocent people, but it would also reveal how easily they themselves could judge others wrongly.

Tales abounded in Maycomb, Alabama, regarding a mysterious, elusive man named Arthur Radley, whom the children called "Boo." Most of the stories were unfounded and untrue. Though they had never met him or even seen him, the children were frightened of him because of this false information.

During that same summer, another scene based on false information saw Atticus enmeshed in a controversial court case involving Tom Robinson, a black man falsely accused of raping a local white man's daughter.

Learning the mystery of Boo Radley and watching their father stand against most of the citizens of Maycomb in defense of an innocent man would prove to be giant steps toward maturity for the children. Their faith in expecting good people to do the right thing would be shattered when Tom Robinson was found guilty. Though all the evidence pointed to Tom's innocence, and though Atticus's defense was overwhelming, the jury was afraid to break the tradition that a black man's word was not accepted above a white man's. Times were changing, however, and Atticus was convinced that an appeal would certainly set Tom free.

Tom never saw that freedom. He was killed trying to escape his misery and discouragement, assured in his mind that injustice would follow injustice, in spite of the truth.

Continuing on his path of vengeance, the vile Bob Ewell, who had forced his daughter to falsely accuse Tom, vowed revenge on the Finch family because of Atticus's defense of a black man. He eventually carried out that vow by attacking Jem and Scout one autumn evening as they were walking home late from a school play.

Unknown to the children at that time, their phantom, Boo Radley, who had so captivated their imagination and who, they were convinced, was seeking to harm them, had kept a careful and secret watch over them for a long time. He saved their lives that night by intercepting their attacker. Scout finally met the mysterious character. To her surprise Boo was not scary at all, nor had he ever posed a threat to anyone—he was a simple-minded, gentle, and shy man who was afraid to be around people. In his simplicity, Boo Radley had come to love Jem and Scout from a distance. Scout learned a very important lesson about "walking around in another person's skin"—that you never judge another person through idle gossip and rumors. Boo was now a treasured friend.

Like the mockingbird, Boo Radley harmed no one. In his own way, he "sang his heart out" for Jem and Scout.

Daniel is another favorite character of mine from the Bible. Even his name exemplified his righteousness. "God is my judge" is the meaning of the name. He knew the pangs of injustice, even from his youth, when he was captured by the Babylonians, separated from his family, and taken to a pagan land to serve in the courts of an ungodly king. Daniel acquiesced to his captivity as God's design for his life and served honorably and faithfully without compromising his own beliefs.

Even as a young man, Daniel was gifted by God with deep wisdom and understanding and was given the ability to interpret visions and dreams. Daniel was also a man of uncompromising standards. His years under various kings had proven him to be blameless, and he was distinguished above all others in the courts of the king "because an excellent spirit was in him" (Daniel 6:3 NKJV).

Jealousy and envy caused the other administrators and princes to seek fault in him, but they failed because Daniel was upright with God and with man. They sought to solve this problem by trapping him in some aspect of his worship. A devious plan was formulated so that King Darius signed into law a decree that anyone praying to any other being except the king for thirty days would be thrown to the lions. Undeterred, Daniel not only prayed to his God but, as usual, did it at an open window. Because the law could not be revoked, King Darius unwillingly relented to Daniel's punishment, even though he realized the honor of his servant Daniel.

Like Tom Robinson of our story above, Daniel faced the cruel injustice of evil men.

Most of us recognize this wonderful story from the Bible and know that God saved Daniel from the lions and that King Darius not only destroyed the wicked accusers of Daniel but their families also.

God may see fit at times to miraculously rescue His children from the throes of fiery trials, but other times He chooses not to do so. I'm sure most of us struggle with the natural emotion of anger at the injustices we see committed against ourselves and others. Righteous indignation is a proper response, but we must remember that God has marked us for adversity in this life, even as our Lord Jesus was marked for adversity.

As did Daniel, who did not know he would survive the lions' den, let us bow to God's sovereignty. God strengthens our souls as we persevere and trust in His wise ways. The angels may not always close the mouths of lions about us, but knowing that nothing touches us except the Lord permits gives us great courage to go forward in the strength of the Lord.

Father, may we seek to understand others
and find that in doing so we
display the compassion of Christ.
Help us to maintain a quiet
dignity and grace as we suffer
the unfairness of this life,
that in all things we bring honor to You.

NOTE

1. Harper Lee, *To Kill a Mockingbird* (Philadelphia: J. B. Lippincott, 1960), 98.
2. Ibid., 36.

God Is
My Hiding Place

You are my hiding place;
you will protect me from trouble
and surround me with
songs of deliverance.

PSALM 32:7

10

PERSECUTION

*The harder blow the stormy winds,
the deeper grow the roots.*

$\mathcal{J}$edem Das Seine" (to each his own) says the stark inscription on the gate to Buchenwald, opening into the darkness of horror of what became one of the largest concentration camps in Germany. Interestingly, the words are inscribed to be read from the inside only. Once in the pages of history, those gates would witness the entrance of untold thousands of the human race upon whom unspeakable atrocities would be inflicted, many of whom would only find freedom again through death.

The year 2000 marked the twentieth anniversary of a very special birthday in the lives of my husband and myself, the cherished occasion of our birth, our spiritual birth, and we traveled back to the country of Germany where that event had taken place. While on this particular trip, we decided to make a visit to the old city of Weimar in eastern Germany. One of the sights we wanted to see was the area of the Buchenwald concentration camp, a few miles north of the city.

Anyone who has ever been to one of these memorial sites knows what an overwhelming cloud of gloom hovers over the entire setting. The shadows of scenes past permeate the air, and the earth seems to scream with the blood of shackled prisoners stripped of any vestige of humanity, the untold suffering of fellow human beings. The atmosphere is one of deep sadness and isolation, as if God has declared a curse upon the land. My own heart was overwhelmed with grief at the thought of such horrible persecution and suffering that had transpired some sixty years ago.

Most people, especially in this country, cannot begin to imagine what real persecution means. There are times when perhaps we are laughed at or humiliated in some fashion, suffering some indignity or injustice because of our beliefs, especially as Christians. But physical abuse, scathing diatribes of verbal abuse, loss of possessions and separation of families, even death, is not a common occurrence we face. When we envision these types of atrocities, it is difficult to conceive of the inhumane capabilities of the perpetrators of such actions.

One group of people who experienced firsthand the inequities of evil men during the Second World War was the ten Boom family. Corrie ten Boom was the youngest child of a devout Christian family in Holland. The ten Booms were not Jewish, the main target of the Nazi regime, nor were they dissidents or criminals or political threats. Their only crime was believing and practicing their faith, adhering to the command of God to "love your neighbor as yourself"—the neighbors, in this case, being the Jewish population. They realized the risks this love would involve but willingly obeyed the God they worshiped to aid the covenant people of Abraham's God.

Father ten Boom was a humble man, a third generation watchmaker, whose grandfather started the family business in a front room of the same house where Corrie's father was born, and where years later, her brother and two sisters, then she, would be born. In the years of her youth, in the city of Haarlem, Corrie learned to serve others by the examples of her mother and father and siblings.

In 1940, when the war was raging all around them, Germany invaded Holland. Within a short time and with little resistance, the country was under the control of the Nazis. The occupation of German troops caused little disruption at first, but progressively the atmosphere filled with tension. Jewish families began to suddenly disappear, businesses closed, homes were vacated, and synagogues burned. Ugly anti-Semitic slogans were painted on public walls. Watches brought in by Jews for repairs began to accumulate in the little ten Boom watch shop.

Corrie, in her book *The Hiding Place,* writes, "Nazism was a disease to which the Dutch too were susceptible, and those with anti-Semitic bias fell sick of it first."[1] Distressed with the alarming reports of deported Jews being killed, the ten Boom family embarked on a dramatic period in their lives, from which there would be no retreat and which would threaten their very existence.

As God orchestrated the circumstances, Corrie became involved with the underground movement to help transport Jews to safety. The movement comprised a large network of people who arranged details of every sort and relocated the dispossessed and persecuted people to establishments of individuals willing to hide and care for them. At first the "hiding place" in the ten Boom home was not used frequently because of its location in the center of the city, but as times and conditions worsened, fewer and fewer places were available to house the Jews. Consequently, the ten Booms ended up with seven new residents, one of whom was a rabbi.

For six months the crowded people of the ten Boom home operated with anxious hearts. Then, in February of 1944, through the betrayal of a fellow Dutchman, the house was raided. Father, now eighty-four years old, sister Betsie, brother Willem, and Corrie were all arrested. Remarkably, the "guests" had successfully made it to the hiding place, and it was so concealed they were not found. The fugitives would later safely escape from their secret place.

Corrie and Betsie were taken to a Dutch prison, and a few months later transported to a camp built for political prisoners in south Holland. The Allied invasion had already begun in Holland. The sisters learned their father had died only ten days after his arrest, before he could get medical help. Because he had no identification papers on him, he was thrown into a nameless grave. Willem had been released.

Because of the closeness of the Allied invasion, the prisoners were taken to Germany, the hated soil of their nightmares, to the dreaded women's extermination camp of Ravensbruck. Deplorable, filthy conditions existed here, stripped of any trace of human regard. In the midst of the crowded stench and brutality, Corrie and her sister were able to minister to countless victims of the war, giving them hope in the Savior they knew and trusted. In that darkness, light shined, and their joy ran deeper than despair.

The camp was liberated at the end of December 1944, but not before Betsie took sick and died. Betsie's vision was for others to know what God had done in this horrible time of history. Corrie honored Betsie's wish, and for years before Corrie's own death, she told the story all over the world of God's faithfulness in an abject time of history.

It is hard to imagine that Christians still suffer for their faith in many parts of the world, even death in many instances. Could we ever foresee a time in the future of our country when persecution of this magnitude might take place? As I stood at the incinerator ovens at Buchenwald, my mind was stunned with the realization of the depth of sin and how easily people fall prey to its clutches. These ovens remained as a grim reminder of that fact.

Yet God was working. Only heaven will reveal the full story. His grace seems to be most beautifully magnified in the lives of His people during their deepest trials. His grace is indeed sufficient, for when we are weak, He is strong. Betsie ten Boom did not dwell on her suffering in a concentration camp; she focused on the goodness of the Lord. As she invoked her sister to tell people what they had learned, she said, "We must tell them that there is no pit so deep that He is not deeper still."

In an age of increasing animosity toward the things of God, when wrong is called right and right is called wrong, it becomes easy to think of history's repeating itself. The fires of hatred are constantly fanned by Satan, and we need to be prepared for his attacks on the followers of Christ. We are blessed in this country with wonderful freedom of worship, and we should take care to praise God for that blessing. We should all remember that we are soldiers; being alert is a command from our Captain. He has given us our weapon for battle, the sword of the Spirit, which is His Word. Let us take constant diligence in being prepared for whatever battle we may be required to enter into—in the strength of His might.

*Father, how blessed we are to be
called servants of the Most High God.
We pray that our words and
actions bring honor to You
when we suffer for His name's sake.
Let us remember Christ suffered
persecution for our salvation.*

NOTE

1. Corrie ten Boom with John and Elizabeth Sherrill, *The Hiding Place* (Uhrichsville, Ohio: Barbour, 1971), 70.

God Is
My Help
and My Hope

Happy is he whose help is the God of Jacob,
whose hope is in the Lord his God,
who made heaven and earth,
the sea, and all that is in them;
who keeps faith for ever;
who executes justice for the oppressed;
who gives food to the hungry.
The Lord sets the prisoners free.

PSALM 146:5–7 RSV

11

ABANDONMENT

*It is not what we do or have done,
not our possessions or beauty or strength.
It is not how others perceive us,
or how we perceive ourselves.
We are of great value because
we are precious to God, who gave us life.*

*H*er name is synonymous with compassion. Mention it and most people will easily recognize who she is. A tiny Albanian named Gonxha, later to be known to the world as Mother Teresa, was a supreme example of the love and compassion of Christ. In deep humility of spirit, she sought to serve her God with all the strength she could give in mind, soul, and body. The outcasts she ministered to were the poorest of the poor in India, abandoned heaps of hopeless souls, left alone to perish among their own filth and disease.

Mother Teresa also symbolized a most important trait of Christ, His love. Love, you see, is the greatest gift of all, for it shows the Savior's face to others. She did not have all knowledge, and many times her faith wavered. Yet she gave all she possessed in this world, surrendering her body as a sacrifice, and she did it with immense love for the poor she sought to serve. Her love was kind and patient; it protected and trusted, was filled with hope, and always persevered amid the severe trials of her environment.

She was taught as a small child to never take a bite of food that she was not willing to share with another. Both her parents showed their children, by example, the true meaning of caring for those less fortunate, so that at a very early age, Gonxha recognized the value of people. They were valuable because God did not care for material things—He cared for people.

As a young teenager Gonxha became intrigued with India and its culture and felt impressed that God wanted her to enter the field of missions. When she sought the advice of a priest as to how she could be sure of her calling, he simply told her that "joy would be her compass." She could think of nothing else that filled her heart with so much joy as would serving the Lord in this strange country.

It was near the end of 1929 when the opportunity came for the young novice to see her dream realized—she was on her way to India. Her heart was horrified to see all the poverty when she first touched the soil of this land— abandoned and neglected souls lying everywhere in rags or nothing at all, many just waiting to die, many already dead. Never had she seen such a sea of human affliction.

Gonxha's training continued as she and the other novices were soon teaching the local boys and girls in the province of Darjeeling. She took the name of Sister Teresa and, during the ensuing two years, began teaching. She also ministered with nurses at small medical stations and the hospital. Sister Teresa related the joy of her experience:

In the hospital pharmacy hangs a picture of the Redeemer surrounded by a throng of suffering people, on whose faces the torments of their lives have been engraved. Each morning, before I start work, I look at this picture. In it is concentrated everything I feel. I think, "Jesus, it is for you and for these souls!" Then I open the door. My heart beats in happiness: I can continue your work, dear Jesus. I can ease many sorrows. I console them and treat them, repeating the words of the best Friend of souls.[1]

The Sister also had the opportunity to begin teaching some of the poorest of the poor children. She discovered the joy she gave to these pitiful creatures by simply touching their dirty little heads. The children affectionately called her "Ma."

While her days were filled with service to others, she had a continual urging within her heart to minister to the poorest of the poor adults as well as the children. By this time she had been named the mother superior of the high school and thus became Mother Teresa. She continued to view the limitations of the convent as a thorn in her side. The still small voice of God was calling Mother Teresa outside the work of her present environment to bring the love of Christ to the abandoned of the streets of Calcutta. She was persistent in her crusade for this ministry because of the deep conviction of God's call to her heart that these unwanted poor needed His love, also.

The challenges were many. Given a year to make it succeed, she ventured out alone, with no funds, to start a new order, calling the work the Missionaries of Charity. Mother

Teresa would need at least ten volunteers to assist her. As she began to minister to the outcasts, people were drawn to her like a magnet. She begged for money to buy food to feed them, but her gentle touch was the most significant emblem of her love. Who ever dared to touch the untouchables? Many, even of her church, referred to her as the "Slum Sister," to which she replied that she was "glad to be just that for His love and glory." Discouragement and insults were her food many days, but still she persevered.

The next few months produced many miracles within Mother Teresa's life. God provided the help she needed and continued to provide over the following years. Her life of self-sacrifice and a simple faith in God produced hundreds of homeless shelters, schools, orphanages, homes for the dying, leper colonies, traveling medical units, and countless volunteers, not just in India but all over the world. When she saw a need, she gave it to God and waited for Him to bring the supply she needed.

How many felt the touch of Jesus through the roughened and calloused hands of one obedient servant? She despised not these creations of God's hand. Jesus touched the unclean. Jesus spoke tenderness to the outcasts of society. Jesus gave them love. He gave them Himself. Jesus was Mother Teresa's example. She could not do less for Him.

When writing his second epistle to Timothy, the beloved apostle Paul must have indeed felt abandoned. Paul was in prison, his friends had deserted him, and he was cold and alone, knowing death would come soon. He wrote in sad and poignant tones to his cherished son in the faith. Still the Lord's faithful servant, he exhorted Timothy to continue in that precious faith. Paul knew he was not alone, as he testified to the fact that the Lord stood by him and gave him strength. The same Lord who had walked with him through all obstacles would also be his escort at his departure from this earth.

Christ still gathers the abandoned ones to Himself. All others may forsake, yet He is near to the brokenhearted who turn their faces in hope to Him. Abandonment may be cloaked in many different guises—the desertion of a mate, family members who no longer care, friends who forsake. It doesn't matter what form of prison we may find ourselves in. God's touch is not confined; it can permeate the deepest pit of one's life. It is in those valleys that our eyes look upward to the consolation of our souls.

Father, when no one's arms hold me close,
let me feel the tender touch of Christ.

NOTE

1. Sam Wellman, *Mother Teresa: Missionary of Charity* (Uhrichsville, Ohio: Barbour, 1997), 51.

The Lord
Is My
Shelter

*Let me live forever
in your sanctuary,
safe beneath the
shelter of your wings!*

— PSALM 61:4 NLT

12

ABUSE

Fraught with care and laden with pain,
he walked the path with teardrops stained;
he breathed the air of suffering.

Scars are a symbol of an inflicted wound. However, many scars are not visible to the naked eye because they are carried in the heart. There are many methods of inflicting wounds, both physically and emotionally. Many times, the physical injury has also injured the heart and spirit. Some memories are the greatest source of debilitating pain that a person can experience, one in which a victim walks in a valley of intense suffering.

We see all around us in the evil of this world the horrible results of physical abuse. Whether it is the abuse of a child or a spouse or even an animal, the marks of this damage are imprinted for a lifetime. Many who have suffered the extreme pain of emotional mistreatment will also carry a permanent stamp of injury deep inside the heart.

Joseph's abusive treatment came from the hands of his brothers—brothers so full of hate and jealousy that they wanted him dead. Joseph's mother had died when he was a young boy, and he had become the apple of his father's eye "because he was the son of his old age." The brothers found the opportunity to be rid of Joseph when, on one occasion, they were absent from home longer than normal tending their father's sheep.

Jacob sent his young son to seek his other sons' whereabouts, but little did he know that this would be their last meeting for many years. Joseph was sold by his siblings to a caravan of traders. From the comfort and security of his father's home and love, Joseph embarked on a journey he could never have imagined. The brothers returned home to their father, telling him that Joseph had been killed by a wild animal.

As the providence of God continued to work out in Joseph's life, he was sold to an officer of Pharaoh who gave him charge of all his household. Because the Lord was with Joseph, he was successful in all he did in his master's house. Joseph was not only the special son of Jacob, but he also was favored in the eyes of his heavenly Father. God's hand was upon Joseph through all the circumstances of his life—the good, the bad, and the ugly. Even as a young man, Joseph recognized the Lord's sovereignty in his life, accepted his condition, and grew in grace and in favor with his God and with those around him.

The ugliness of abuse reared its head again as the wife of Potiphar tried to seduce the handsome Joseph. Joseph's integrity would not let him commit such an evil act against the Lord he loved and served, and so he fled from her presence. The spurned would-be adulteress lied to her husband and accused Joseph of trying to attack her. Joseph was cast into another pit, this time the prison of the king.

Again, we find that "the Lord was with Joseph and showed him steadfast love and gave him favor in the sight of the keeper of the prison" (Genesis 39:21 RSV).

This "dreamer" interpreted dreams for the baker and the cupbearer of the pharaoh. When the cupbearer was released, as Joseph had foretold in his interpretation, Joseph implored his help to escape his unjust imprisonment. His kindness to these men was quickly forgotten, and for another two years, Joseph remained in prison.

When Pharaoh had a terrible dream that his wise men could not interpret for him, his cupbearer suddenly remembered Joseph. Joseph was released, and he rendered to the king not only the meaning of the dream but also the solution to the problem it presented. A period of seven years of plenty followed by seven years of famine would come upon all the land, and he proposed the stockpiling of grain for the years of plenty to enable the nation to survive during the time of famine.

Pharaoh was so impressed by Joseph's wisdom that he placed him second in command of the entire country. So God continued to give his faithful servant favor in the eyes of all those around him.

Joseph was given a wife, and God blessed them with two sons, the names of whom indicate the trust he had in the Lord. Manasseh showed that "God has made me forget all my hardship and all my father's house," and Ephraim expressed that "God has made me fruitful in the land of my affliction" (Genesis 41:51–52 RSV). His abuse had worked in his life for his enrichment and to bring honor to God.

Joseph certainly had not forgotten his father—I'm sure his heart yearned to see his father's face—but God had made him forget the pain that was inflicted upon his body and heart by his brothers. Joseph did not seek vengeance; he understood that God would take care of the wrongs done to him even though, while enduring the mistreatment, he did not understand God's reasons for allowing them.

The story has a happy ending, for the brothers who so despicably used Joseph had to seek help in Egypt during the famine. The dreams Joseph had dreamed as a young man would be realized when his siblings, unable to recognize him after so many years, bowed before him in obeisance as they asked for grain from this ruler of Egypt. Joseph tested his brothers' motives and intentions, but eventually he brought all of his family, along with his beloved father, to live near him for the rest of his life.

Joseph comprehended God's overruling providence in the situations of life, his life as well as the lives of all people. He was chosen for God's perfect purposes in God's perfect timing, just as we are. He later told his brothers when they were frightened as they learned his identity, "God sent me before you to preserve for you a remnant on earth, and to keep alive for you many survivors. So it was not you who sent me here, but God" (Genesis 45:7–8 RSV). And later, after their father died, he told them clearly, "As for you, you meant evil against me; but God meant it for good, to bring it about that many people should be kept alive, as they are today" (Genesis 50:20 RSV).

You see, scars are also a symbol of healing—where

once a gaping wound existed, only the impression remains, and the pain imposed by that blow can hardly be remembered. Even in the valley of our affliction, God can make us fruitful for His use if we lay our burdens upon Him. Some carry more scars than others, and it is easy to pick out those whose wounds have been yielded to Christ. Jesus suffered along with us, and He has Himself borne our sorrows and our griefs. The scars He will carry for eternity remind His children of that great sacrifice.

Moses admonished the children of Israel to remember how the Lord had been with them through all their wanderings in the wilderness. As they were about to enter the land God had promised to them, he told them God would fight for them, even as He had in the desert. He reminded them, "There you saw how the LORD your God carried you, as a father carries his son, all the way you went until you reached this place" (Deuteronomy 1:31).

In our wanderings on this earth, God still bears us through whatever wilderness of pain we might travel.

Father, cover the wounds of
my heart and spirit with the
healing ointment of the Cross.
May my scars remind me of that
which the Savior suffered for my sake.

God Is
My Healer

But for you who fear my name,
the Sun of Righteousness will rise
with healing in his wings.

— MALACHI 4:2 NLT

13

ADDICTION

Prone to wander, Lord, I feel it,
Prone to leave the One I love;
Here's my heart, O take and seal it;
Seal it for Thy courts above.
(ROBERT ROBINSON)

*Y*ears ago addiction could be defined in a much more narrow way than it can be today—it was the uncontrolled habit of and physical dependence on drugs or alcohol. In this age of advancement, however, the definition has broadened considerably to a more generalized meaning of behavioral excess. Addiction is rampant and widespread and encompasses a wide spectrum of obsessions, from sex and pornography to eating and excessive spending. Many things hold the capability to be addictive and, though we seldom think of the dangers, none of us is exempt from entrapment.

The amusements and practices of the world are made to be attractive to us. We are constantly told by the world of advertising that we *must* have these things or do these things to be happy and fulfilled. Like Eve tempted by the serpent in the Garden of Eden, our eyes feast upon an object or an activity, our minds are engaged into the desire for it, and we are hooked. Of course, we can always rationalize that there is nothing wrong with wanting to possess certain items, to be fashionable and trendy, or to participate in various endeavors.

Most objects and activities are not in themselves wrong, but the Bible states, "For you are a slave to whatever controls you" (2 Peter 2:19 NLT). The apostle Paul told the Corinthian believers in 1 Corinthians 6:12, "'Everything is permissible for me'—but not everything is beneficial. 'Everything is permissible for me'—but I will not be mastered by anything." It is not the object or activity that is necessarily sin—it is the enslavement, or obsession, that becomes the sin. Many people have enslaved themselves to hard taskmasters, and we all need to realize how easy it is to fall into the valley of obsession and excess.

The drug addict, alcoholic, or gambler did not know that he would eventually fall prey to the substance or habit he first submitted to. Such is the subtlety of sin—we are overpowered before we realize it. The habit becomes our master instead of us controlling the habit. And the popular trend of calling the addiction an illness instead of sin only adds to the struggle for recovery. When a person has an illness, he cannot be held responsible for personal actions related to it. There can, of course, in many cases of addiction, be physically related illnesses and problems associated with the addiction. But the addiction itself is not an illness.

The Bible stresses moderation in all things; excessive, compulsive, and obsessive behavior is sinful. Sin must be acknowledged and repented of before one can be forgiven —and before he can be provided the right frame of mind to overcome the obsession. It is when we realize that we have acted against God that there is hope for overcoming the addiction.

So much in life can detract from a believer's spiritual growth. Even innocent things—things we would never consider addictive—taken to excess can become an overpowering hindrance to the Holy Spirit's work in our hearts. The pursuit of material things and pleasure have indeed become obsessions with many people. Certainly God has given us all things to enjoy, but when materialism and pleasure become monumental in a life, they expose self-centeredness within the heart and obscure the true purpose God intended those things to have. It also blights Christians' testimony to the world when we appear to be no different from the world.

A quick study in the life of Lot traces the story of one obsessed with the things of the world. The story of Abraham's nephew takes place in the book of Genesis. The sketch of Lot that the Bible gives us is enough that we can see where his treasure lay.

Over the course of time, Abraham and Lot had accrued great wealth. Their combined riches began to create dissension between the herdsmen of the two men because the land was not spacious enough for their flocks to dwell together. Abraham knew that to have peace, he and Lot would have to separate.

Being the gracious man he was, he gave Lot the option to choose which way he would go—Abraham would take the opposite of Lot's choice. The Bible says, "And Lot lifted his eyes and saw all the plain of Jordan, that it was well watered everywhere" (Genesis 13:10 NKJV). Lot proceeded on his journey to the good land before him and set up camp near the wicked city of Sodom. A sad phrase echoes in this section of the chapter: "And they separated from each other" (13:11 NKJV).

Lot looked and desired the land for himself—he was committed to obtaining his desire. Apparently Lot's wealth had given him a good life, and he wanted more of it. The stable and godly influence of his uncle had been a shelter for him. Now he was content to venture away from that sanctuary.

The latter part of the story is truly pitiful and should pose a grim warning to each of us. Lot's choice of the well-watered land of the Jordan drew him finally into the wicked city of Sodom itself. We have no reason to doubt that the notoriety of Sodom was known to Lot. Yet he chose to live close to the brink and then was sucked into the environs of wickedness.

Lot married and raised two daughters within the confines of Sodom, and Peter tells us in the New Testament that "his righteous soul 'was' vexed" (2 Peter 2:8 KJV). What a grievous thing to be in the midst of wickedness, condemned in soul, and yet continue to remain in evil's grip. We see as the story progresses, God pronounced judgment on the cities of Sodom and Gomorrah. The Lord graciously informed His friend Abraham of the impending doom.

Because of the pious entreaties of Abraham to the Lord, He spared the lives of Lot and his family. As this chapter of Lot's life ends, we see the angels physically forcing Lot and his wife and two daughters from the city.

Reluctantly, as they departed this "good life," Lot's wife could not resist the temptation to look back at the condemned city, though the angels had specifically told them not to. As a result she was turned into a pillar of salt.

The harvest of seeking after the things of the world was that Lot's life concluded in misery and shame. He lost all his worldly possessions, his wife was gone, and he ended up living in fear in a cave with his daughters. Those daughters, influenced by the evil of their environment and the wickedness of their hearts, got their father drunk and each conceived a child by him. These children became the fathers of two great enemies—the Edomites and the Moabites—of the Israelites.

Such was the life of Lot. A pathetic testimony of someone who was given so much by God, yet lived with an indifference to His commandments. How would we have ever known Lot was a righteous man if we had not been told in 2 Peter 2:8?

The story of Lot and his family may seem extreme, but it serves as a serious reminder of how easy it is to be slowly drawn into lifestyles unpleasing to God. All of us are susceptible, and many of us fall into the trap. The greatest problem is the problem of the heart, where the desire of the passion is rooted. When the root is removed, with God's help, the person can then experience the power to overcome those things that tempt and enslave him.

Believers have been granted this power by God, as 2 Peter 1:3 tells us: "His divine power has given us everything we need for life and godliness through our knowledge of him who called us by his own glory and goodness."

Peter further tells us that this power enables us to over-come and escape the "corruption in the world caused by evil desires." As servants of Christ we are commanded to live holy and godly lives, and the Lord has granted the re-sources to do so. With God's help and the help of compas-sionate Christians to come alongside, recovery can become a reality for the addict.

> *Lord, we realize how prone we are*
> *to wander from Your commandments.*
> *Give us insight into our hearts*
> *that we may surrender those objects*
> *and delights of our affections*
> *that are displeasing to You.*
> *May our hearts be enslaved*
> *only to our Master, the Lord Jesus.*

God Is
My Fortress

Lead me to the towering rock of safety,
for you are my safe refuge,
a fortress where my
enemies cannot reach me.

PSALM 61:2–3 NLT

14

TRAGEDY

A mighty fortress is our God,
A bulwark never failing.
(MARTIN LUTHER)

Death separates and death unites. Death separates loved ones and friends; death unites those left behind, for grief is a common thread whereby all humanity is bonded.

On December 8, 1941, President Franklin Roosevelt declared, "Yesterday, December 7, 1941—a date which will live in infamy—the United States of America was suddenly and deliberately attacked by naval and air forces of the empire of Japan." In less than one hour from his announcement, both houses of Congress unanimously approved a declaration of war.

Pearl Harbor had suffered a tremendous loss of warships, but the greatest toll was the death of some twenty-four hundred American soldiers. The Secretary of the Navy had boasted only a few days prior to the bombing that the U.S. Navy would not be "caught napping." However, as was evidenced on that terrible day, the Navy, as well as the population of America, was totally unsuspecting.

Under the leadership of President Roosevelt, America

had slowly been emerging from the ravages of the Great Depression, and its people, up until that fateful day in December, had no interest in entering another world war being fought on foreign soil. December 7 changed all that —the enemy opened the gate to a united resolve to enact justice. The attack had brought about the "forging of an unprecedented degree of unity in the U.S." What a difference a day makes!

The war persisted almost four more years, and the casualty total of American military lives numbered over 300,000. The cost of freedom is very dear and touches millions of people.

During another tumultuous time in our nation, a man whose life had been subjected to tremendous personal sorrows assumed the office of the presidency of a country about to be plunged into a deep abyss of untold misery. It seemed appropriate that God had prepared just the man for this time in the history of the United States, for only one who had himself experienced deep sorrow could in turn offer comfort and compassion and hope to those about to be subjected to the same.

Even the road to the White House was marred with controversy and fear, and from the time Abraham Lincoln was elected in November of 1860 until he assumed the office in March of 1861, eight states seceded from the Union. Within a few short weeks after his taking office, the bloodiest battle on the soil of our country was about to begin.

The War Between the States was a war of a nation divided. More than six hundred thousand lives were lost in a conflict that pitted brother against brother and neighbor against neighbor. The most bloody battle of the Civil War, resulting in the most lives lost in one day, was fought on September 17, 1862, at Antietam, Maryland.

On September 11, 2001, another infamous day occurred. The destruction of the World Trade Center buildings in New York City and an attack on the Pentagon in Washington, D.C., were perpetrated by terrorists against the United States. These "suicide attackers" hijacked commercial planes and coordinated unthinkable acts of destruction by flying them into the buildings, amassing not only the devastation of the facilities but the annihilation of untold numbers of innocent lives.

Lives of the passengers and crew members aboard the airplanes were lost, in addition to people working within the buildings. Firemen and policemen called to the emergency ended up losing their lives also. Another plane, which intelligence agents believe may have been headed for the Capitol building or the White House, was obstructed from its target by a few brave passengers who probably attacked the terrorists and caused the plane to crash in a field.

As the horror of that morning unfolded before the eyes of Americans within the brief span of a few hours, something dramatic outside of the incidents themselves emerged—people began uniting in one spirit and one heart. Suddenly, "others" took on a greater importance. Things once taken for granted were thrust to the forefront of people's minds and hearts. Patriotism was the watchword of the day, and citizens rose to the occasion. Stories of sacrifice and heroism abounded.

Millions of Americans awoke that Tuesday morning with the assumption that that day would be another normal day in their lives. Within a few hours all of us realized, however, that life would never be the same again for any of us. The carnage amassed with such swiftness was inconceivable. We stared in shock, overwhelmed at the reality of the moment, and wept.

Tragedy. Sudden, rapid, sure. Inflicted upon the unsuspecting. And propelling those involved into a future of uncertainty. It causes people to rearrange their priorities and compels them to realize that death is no respecter of persons. It can happen at any time, at any place, to any people, under any circumstance. No one is immune.

What is certain in this life? For the believer, there is One who is our certainty; One who knows all and controls all; One who is not taken by surprise when tragedy occurs; and One, even in the midst of the chaos of our lives, who is working in all things for our good and His glory. Even in turmoil, God speaks in a still, small voice to those with ears that can hear. The wrath of nature, of war and devastation, of death and suffering, all display the mercies of God.

The prophet Elijah experienced the turmoil of war, of famine, of fear. In fleeing from the wicked Queen Jezebel, he hid in a cave in the mountain of Horeb. Discouraged and afraid for his life, he cried out to God. God graciously and lovingly instructed Elijah, "Go out and stand before me on the mountain."

As Elijah stood there, the Lord passed by, and a mighty windstorm hit the mountain. It was such a terrible blast that the rocks were torn loose, but the Lord was not in the wind. After the wind there was an earthquake, but the Lord was not in the earthquake. And after the earthquake there was a fire, but the Lord was not in the fire. And after the fire there was the sound of a gentle whisper. When Elijah heard it, he wrapped his face in his cloak and went out and stood at the entrance of the cave. (1 Kings 19:11–13 NLT)

God uses the tragedies of our lives to turn our hearts to Himself, the only true source of peace and calm in the midst of chaos. When a weary one lies sleepless in the darkness and silence of the night, after the voices of the day subside and the reality of disaster settles heavy upon the heart, God still speaks in a still, small voice, "Come to me, all you who are weary and burdened, and I will give you rest. Take my yoke upon you and learn from me, for I am gentle and humble in heart, and you will find rest for your souls" (Matthew 11:28–29).

*Father, help us to rest in
the assurance of Your love.
Though we don't understand
so many of life's heartaches,
help us to know Your purposes are perfect.
Let us rest our weary hearts
upon the breast of our gentle Lord.*

Part Three

VALLEYS
of the
HEART

God Is
My Defense

He only is my rock
and my salvation;
He is my defense;
I shall not be greatly moved.

PSALM 62:2 NKJV

15

BETRAYAL

Seasons lost in the chasm
of "could have been"
remind of the footprints
taken on the pathway
to the gate of "never to be."

Who would ever have thought it? *Why is this happening to me?* Terrie asked herself these questions as she tried to sort out the words she had just heard her husband say.

On a vacation trip they took, she made a desperate attempt to find out why their relationship was deteriorating, threatening a divorce unless he explained to her what was going on with him. When he asked her what *she* thought, she blurted out all the horrors that had gone through her mind over the previous several months. "You've been married before. You've found someone else. You have a child I don't know about. You've killed someone. Or," something she had not considered before, "maybe you've had a homosexual experience."

Nothing prepared her for his response. "I'm gay" was the deafening answer.

She was dazed with disbelief. As she clutched him, trying to awaken from this nightmare, she grew numb from the shock of his confession. How could she handle something like this?

The next few days were a blur—the jolt of his confession had paralyzed her. They cut short their vacation trip, and when they arrived home the truth hit her. It was the first time she had been able to completely release the agony that had built up inside her. When the dam burst, the wails of her cries were described by her husband as those of a wounded animal in the deep forest.

Terrie didn't know how they would work this out, but she never doubted that they could and would. She loved her husband and the children who had been born of that love, and when the reality of his confession began to sink in, she set about trying desperately to save her marriage and family. She fought alone to keep her home intact, concealing the shameful secret from her children and other family members. After two years and three counselors, and many anguished tears and prayers, Terrie's husband of thirteen years made the decision to leave his wife and children for good.

Betrayal. The word carries a repulsive idea. To turn one's back on, to fail or desert in time of need, to become a traitor, the mark of a Judas kiss. All these ugly words defining an ugly act. Betrayal wears many faces, whether it is from a spouse, a family member, a friend, a business associate, even a Christian sister or brother. It wounds deeply because it is inflicted by someone you trust, someone you may have confided in, someone you love. It can impose a grief that is overwhelming.

Betrayal leaves in its wake broken hearts and lasting

scars. The recipient of betrayal is usually left with a sense of bewilderment in addition to the grief, a feeling of having been the prey of the unexpected. So often the victim stands alone with a guilty sense of causing the problem.

In an interesting interjection inserted into the book of Genesis between the story of the betrayal of Joseph by his brothers and Joseph's life in Egypt, we find the tale of Tamar.

Judah, one of the sons of Jacob, married a Canaanite woman and fathered three sons. When he was of age, Er, Judah's oldest son, was wed to a young woman named Tamar. Er, however, was wicked, and the Lord took his life. In ancient Hebrew law, it was appropriate for the second son to take his brother's widow and raise up descendants in his brother's name. Onan, this second son, took Tamar as his wife but was not willing to father a child who would not be his own. Again, this wicked refusal displeased the Lord, and He struck down Onan.

Tamar was instructed to return to her father's house until Judah's third son, Shelah, was old enough to marry her. To return to her father's household, widowed twice and childless, was a deep humiliation for this young woman, but she had no choice. Little did Tamar know that Judah had no intentions of allowing Shelah to marry her, for he feared that his final son's life would be taken, also. Time passed, and Tamar finally realized Judah would not honor his commitment to her.

Perhaps during the period that she had lived with the family of Judah, Tamar came to know about the strange God of Judah's father, Jacob, and their peculiar method of worship. Perhaps Judah had left his own father because of the guilt and shame he felt at having helped to sell his younger, innocent brother into slavery. We can surmise a lot, although the Bible doesn't give us details in this regard. We do know that Hebrew law strictly forbade the marriage of an Israelite to any person from the heathen nations around them. Indeed, Judah had wandered far away from the God of his father. But even living in a pagan land, apart from God, Judah would find God's hand on his life, even in his disobedience.

Judah had lost two sons, and in the course of time, his wife also died. After a period of mourning, he went down to the town to supervise the shearing of his sheep. After waiting so long for her rightful dues and being disappointed at Judah's ignoring those rights, Tamar decided to take things into her own hands. Upon finding out that he was coming to town, she dressed as a prostitute and sat beside the road at the entrance to the village, disguising herself with a veil. Tamar enticed Judah to lie with her, and she got pregnant.

Later, when he heard his daughter-in-law had played the harlot and was with child, the self-righteous Judah was adamant that she be killed. Then Tamar sent to Judah his own seal, cord, and staff that he had given her as a pledge for payment to sleep with her. Realizing he was caught in his own deception, Judah acknowledged his lack of his rightful provision for Tamar and admitted that he was responsible for her pregnancy.

God's Word is so rich with the descriptions of the realism of His people—their frailties as well as their strengths. He chooses as most of us would not choose. For through the betrayal of Tamar and through Judah's improper relationship with her came the birth of twin boys, one of whom (Perez) would be another link in the genealogy chain to our Lord Jesus Christ. We are given hope and encouragement that God has taken not the kings and princes of the world as heirs of His kingdom but some of the most vile and foolish to accomplish His purposes.

Christ has also promised His children that nothing can separate us from His love although all others may forsake us. Terrie's valley has been deep and lonely, yet she knows she is not alone. Beneath the crushing weight of her grief, for her own broken heart and for her children, her faith has sustained her. She is committed to love God and trust Him in spite of her emotions and circumstances. Though her love for her husband was rejected and betrayed, she knows Christ has given her the strength to continue on.

Terrie's story has traumatic consequences. Not only is she affected, but her children also suffer the loss of a father and the aftermath of his choices. This young woman has been through fiery conflicts. I love the Bible passage that she claims as an infallible promise: "Our God whom we serve is able to deliver us from the burning fiery furnace, and he will deliver us out of thine hand, O king. But if not, be it known unto thee, O king, that we will not serve thy gods, nor worship the golden image which thou hast set up" (Daniel 3:17–18 KJV).

God used this "furnace" of her life to refine her, and Terrie's desire is that her life will reflect God's faithfulness. She prays that her testimony will help and encourage others facing similar situations, realizing that God's sweet grace is sufficient for every circumstance of life, no matter how hard.

Those who have traveled along the same kind of pathway and have felt their lives crumble into utter shambles because they have been crushed in heart can find hope in the God who takes the ashes of our lives and makes things of beauty from them.

Father, though all others fail us,
even those closest to our hearts,
help us to remember Your faithfulness.
Let us seek refuge in You when
our lives are shattered with pain.

God Is
My Dwelling Place

*For you have made the Lord,
my refuge, even the Most High,
your dwelling place. No evil
will befall you, nor will any
plague come near your tent.*

PSALM 91:9–10 NASB

16

PULLING UP ROOTS

Time, where did it go?
Moments turn quickly into memories.
Tomorrow soon vanishes into yesterday,
and today cries because she is no more.

*H*ome has been defined in many ways. It has been said that home is where the heart is. Home is where you hang your hat. Home is a light in the window. The definition I like best says that home is in the bosom of one's family. Whatever we call it, all of us have our own sense of what that word means. To some it identifies something very precious; to others it may be something sad or even painful. No matter our view, the homes we grew up in and the homes we are now a part of have significant import in who we are.

I grew up in a rural area in South Carolina and can't remember the thought ever occurring to me that one day I would move away from all things that were familiar to me, nor do I think I ever desired to do so. All that changed shortly after high school when I got married. Our first move carried us to a university city where my husband would complete his degree. Although our move took us only a few short hours from our hometown, for me it seemed a great distance. Little did I realize that this would be the first of many relocations for us, most of which would take us great distances from the state of our births.

I think I actually enjoyed relocating at first. Probably because I had traveled so little during my life, I found it interesting. After our daughter was born and I no longer worked outside the home, my life took on a different dimension. My circle of friends was comprised of my neighbors and those with whom Bill, my husband, worked.

Then with each move that we made with his company, which seemed to occur every two to three years, I began to ache each time we had to pack up and leave. Saying good-bye to those who had become good friends was extremely hard, not to mention saying good-bye to a house that was finally beginning to feel like home, our home.

As time passed and we added a son to our family, and as the children grew older and started school, it became increasingly difficult to take them away from familiarity. Being without the Lord at that time in our lives, our priorities were quite different than they would be several years later. The deep effect that being uprooted had on the children, and on me, was emotionally upsetting. I no longer wanted close relationships since I knew sooner or later I would have to leave them. It began to be a very lonely time. I had all the material things that anyone could wish, yet my life was empty, both emotionally and spiritually.

By God's mercy and intervention in our lives twenty years ago when we were living in Germany, we found new purpose and meaning for our existence in Him. Our moving experiences were not over yet, but now those moves were for His purposes and not ours. The Lord taught us many lessons in the ensuing years.

I realize that in God's divine plan for our lives, He allowed those experiences for a purpose, some of which I would never trade. Our lives have been enriched by so many of the people we have met and the places we have lived. Yet I still have a keen sense of missing something very special when I talk to friends who have lived in the same area all their lives.

Many years ago, there was another young woman in the throes of being uprooted. Bereft of husband and childless, Ruth lived with an embittered mother-in-law who had come to the land of Moab with her husband and two sons. Naomi's husband had died and her sons married Moabite women. Then those sons also died.

When this mother-in-law decided to return to her homeland, she instructed her daughters-in-law to return to their own people. One of them did, but Ruth felt such fierce loyalty and love for her mother-in-law that she was willing to leave all that was familiar to go with Naomi. The young woman replied, "Don't ask me to leave you and turn back. I will go wherever you go and live wherever you live. Your people will be my people, and your God will be my God. I will die where you die and will be buried there. May the Lord punish me severely if I allow anything but death to separate us" (Ruth 1:16–17 NLT)!

Ruth left everything familiar to face an unknown land, an unknown people, an unknown future, and a place where, quite possibly, she might be ostracized because of her race. Her love was bound to her mother-in-law, Naomi, not to her address. And it is evident from reading of her life that she had also bound herself to the God of the Hebrews. The poignant story of her devotion and love is unmatched.

One can never outgive God. The One in whom Ruth trusted took care of this young widow and her mother-in-law. They were accepted into the neighborhood in Bethlehem, as Naomi's friends learned of Ruth's tender love for her. As she sought to care for Naomi and herself, Ruth was placed, by the providence of God, to glean in the fields of Boaz, a wealthy and righteous kinsman of Naomi's husband. She had no knowledge of his identity at that time but was thankful for the kindness he showed her. Ruth would eventually marry Boaz and become one of the links in the genealogy of our Lord Jesus.

As I read and reread the wonderful stories of the lives of God's people in the Bible, I have learned that there are usually many lessons we can gather. The little book of Ruth in the Old Testament is obviously more than just the message of the displacement of an obscure Moabitess from her homeland. It is a story of devotion and love and of the redeeming grace of God.

Through Ruth's chronicle, I can also trace the Lord's hand on my life as I moved from place to place, through the difficulties of transition and upheaval, through the span of distance from families, through the resettlement in strange places, and through the sadness for what was left behind. I have come to realize that what God orchestrates in my life serves a purpose beyond what I can sometimes

understand, but is always for my good. One thing is certain
—there will be a day when my true home will be settled
forever in heaven with Him.

Father, we are pilgrims on this earth.
Set our vision on our true home in heaven.
The times of uprooting here may bring us sadness,
but let our hearts contemplate our
everlasting home where separations will cease.

The Lord
Is My
Keeper

The Lord is thy keeper:
the Lord is thy shade
upon thy right hand.

— PSALM 121:5 KJV

17

BEING A CAREGIVER

*Your kindness may be the only cup of water
a panting soul may drink today.
Give freely.*

*A*s a child it was one of the joys of my life to visit my maternal grandparents. Sunday afternoons were special times when we visited them. My grandfather was a farmer, and my older brother and I spent hours playing in the big barn with the loft full of hay. Summers were wonderful when we were able to spend weeks at a time with our grandparents.

My grandpa died when I was eight years old, and my grandmother lived another ten years. When I was a senior in high school, she suffered a stroke that left her a total invalid. She also lost her capability to speak. Up until that time, Gramma had lived with my uncle and his family, but after her stroke, she came to live with my family.

My mother cared for my grandmother as one cares for a small child. Gramma was totally dependent on my mother. As a teenager, I'm sure I did not realize how difficult it was for my mother. There were still four children at home, and even though caring for her mother was a true act of love for my mom, the added burden of caring for an invalid parent was great. The strain of watching her mother in such a state also took an emotional toll.

It was also a time of stress for our family as a whole. A sudden unexpected illness or accident creates a lot of emotional and physical strain for those involved. When you love the person who is sick or incapacitated, the sorrow runs deep. I have often thought of my grandmother's being unable to communicate, and I realize the difficulty it must have been for her also. She had been independent most of her life. Now she needed someone to assist her in the simplest of tasks.

As time progressed, the tasks of each day became routine. But there was almost always the atmosphere of sadness. We recognized that, unless a miracle occurred, finality of life approached daily. When that day arrived, even though it was expected, the grief was still very acute.

My mom, of course, felt the hardest impact of Gramma's death. For almost a year, she had attended to her mother's needs as well as the needs of her family. Now she had to try to adjust to a life of normalcy once again.

This would not be the only time in my mom's life that she would care for the physical needs of another. Several years later my dad was involved in a terrible car accident in which he almost lost his life. As a result he was totally disabled. It was another traumatic time for our family. After two months of intensive hospital care, he came home, left to the care of my mother. This time, however, there were other complications—medical needs to be administered such as feeding and breathing tubes. My dad was also much larger than my grandmother had been, and though my mother was strong physically, she was older now.

Again, it was a time of waiting for the inevitable. Eight months later my dad passed away, and again life assumed another change of pace. This time was different, however. My mother was now a widow, and I knew her life would never be the same.

It is not an uncommon practice to become the caregiver of someone you love. Since we live with all the uncertainties of this life, most of us will probably come to a point of decision in which we will be that caregiver or, in some cases where that may not be possible, we must place the loved one in the care of others. Those decisions are not always easy. It is heartbreaking for families and generally also for the one who is the recipient of the care. The caregiver often is so involved with the needs of the patient that much of everything else must be put to the side.

Dr. Robertson McQuilkin, former president of Columbia University in South Carolina, made a dramatic decision regarding the care of his wife, who was diagnosed with Alzheimer's in 1978. He did not consider his decision dramatic, however. After assessing the situation and figuring he could never repay his wife for all her years of devotion and care of him, he felt that the decision to resign his position to tend to her needs was one of the easiest he had ever made.

Mrs. McQuilkin, whom her husband refers to as his precious Muriel, had an early onset of Alzheimer's at the age of fifty-five. There would be a few more years before she began to need constant care, but one of the first signs of the disease was her fright when her husband was not with her. His presence calmed her. It was difficult for Dr. McQuilkin to watch his beloved as this terrible menace slowly diminished her mental faculties. In his book *A Promise Kept,* he recounts,

> There is that subterranean grief that won't go away. It increases daily as the lights go out. As Alzheimer's slowly locked away one part of my Muriel, then another, every loss for her shut down a part of me. There was another sense of loss, however, an unassuageable ache deep inside, as I watched my vivacious companion of the years slip from me.[1]

Muriel would not notice the changes as much. Her contentment was being in the presence of her companion. The ensuing years were a definite learning experience for the college president as Muriel depended more and more on him, but he pursued those years with vigor and determination and an ever deepening love for his wife. He was wonderfully surprised by the discovery that his efforts to care for her were not burdensome. He did not feel confined or deprived by his decision to care for Muriel but rather was given a freedom to grow deeper in love.

Of course there were times of frustration and sadness, but Dr. McQuilkin's love and trust in his heavenly Father and his devotion to his Precious made those moments bearable. He understood God's design for his life and did not need to ask unanswerable questions. Many friends who encouraged him to place Muriel in a nursing home could not understand *his* need for her and his joy and contentment in caring for her. He learned more and more each day to praise God in all things and learned that "the heavy heart lifts on the wings of praise."

Dr. McQuilkin never considered himself a victim, as many would call themselves in the same situation, nor would he describe his wife in such a manner. His attitude was one of joy and thanksgiving in being fortunate enough to merit this position. He had learned that God indeed works His power and contentment in lives fully submitted to Him.

Jesus was the compassionate One who took pity on the weak and infirm, on the diseased and disabled, on the outcast and unlovely. He was the ultimate caregiver, and while He walked this earth His days were filled with caring for others—tending His small band of disciples, who were sometimes dull of understanding, sometimes void of reason, sometimes fearful. He healed the many sick and feeble, fed multitudes, calmed fears, encouraged hearts, strengthened the weak, and gave hope to the hopeless. Our Savior took upon Himself the cares and burdens of we humans, who could not carry the load ourselves.

He continues that work today in His people. That's why we are told to cast all our burdens on Him. That's the reason that someone like Dr. McQuilkin can find such peace and joy in his situation. That's how my mother had the strength to provide loving care for my grandmother and my dad. And that is the way that God's children can see His hand working in all areas of our lives so that we can rejoice in all circumstances.

Father, in our care for others,
may they feel Your kind hand through us.
May that which others see as
our prison walls become to us
a beautiful garden because You are there.

NOTE

1. Robertson McQuilkin, *A Promise Kept: The Story of an Unforgettable Love* (Wheaton, Ill.: Tyndale, 1998), 85.

God Is
My Hope

For God alone
my soul waits in silence,
for my hope is from him.

~ PSALM 62:5 RSV

18

THE WAYWARD CHILD

*Time was, when a tiny soul,
clothed with flesh and bone
entered my life and carved
its image upon my heart.
What lies ahead? asks my heart.*

Rearing children has always been a challenge, especially today when so many idols of the world abound, offering temptations of every kind to win their hearts. For Christians, finding the balance in dealing with decisions of what to allow our children to be involved with is not as easy as we would like. Some of those directives are obvious, of course, but others, parents wrestle with. Friends, fashion, music, movies and entertainment, videos, books, and a host of other issues are frequent concerns that cause conflicts between parent and child. Concerns among children now are much more intense and confusing than they were twenty or thirty years ago.

We are sobered to find that suicide is the number one cause of death among teenagers. Our kids are looking for meaning to their lives and a place to belong. When the home does not afford those elements, they search elsewhere. Most of the time, it is in the wrong places. Even in the best of environments, it is tough growing up. Good, nurturing parents often are confronted with situations that they are at a loss to handle.

Many children, wanting independence, will display defiance toward our authority, and thus toward the Lord. These may be "good" kids trying to make the statement "I know how to handle myself." Of course, the reality is, they usually don't. Wisdom is typically slow in developing in most people, especially children, but there comes a time in their lives when parents play the secondary role in their opinions about boundaries.

Boundaries are at the top of the confrontational battle. Kids don't want to be told what or what not to do, especially if their friends have no restraints. Many times parents are worn down in battle simply through frustration. It's tough to show "tough love."

I am often amazed as I read and reread passages of Scripture, especially those that are very familiar to me. The story recorded in Luke 15:11–32 is one such illustration, commonly referred to as the "Prodigal Son." I recently came to realize that nowhere in the passage is the word *prodigal* used—not even in the King James Version.

Another discovery I made was the meaning of the word. Generally I associated the definition with *wayward,* but Webster's Dictionary gives the meaning, derived from the Latin root, as "to drive away" or "squander," which is what the son of course did. It further defines the word as synonymous with the word *profuse,* meaning "pouring forth liberally or without restraint" or "reckless lavishness threatening to lead to early exhaustion of resources." This discovery certainly did not change the meaning of the story at all, but it gave me a deeper insight into it.

The wayward son in the gospel of Luke is a classic example of a child whose heart had not been surrendered to the Lord. His thoughts were centered upon himself and the pleasure he desired. In our imaginations, we can envision the boy surrounding himself with the wrong kinds of friends and influences. It is not so hard for us to picture this lad of biblical days in the throes of today's society, demanding his independence and "rights."

I know the story depicts God's love for His wandering children and His yearning for their return. But it also reveals a realistic display of ordinary family disputes, including sibling problems. The father's heart obviously was broken, though I have often wondered why he chose to give the son what he wanted. The son was certainly not entitled to his inheritance before his father died. Perhaps the father knew, or at least surmised, that the foolishness of his son would be the channel to awaken his senses. Perhaps this was his full surrender of his son to God, trusting his heavenly Father for the results.

The wanderer was certainly *profuse* in his use of his possessions as well as in his behavior, for he did not take long to squander all on partying, drinking, and sex. His older brother later accused the father of allowing the younger son to "squander" the father's living. When all his assets were spent, the boy was left destitute of friend and spirit. To add to his problems, a severe famine came to the land and no one came to help him. This is a true portrayal of the famine that comes upon the hearts and minds of children who have made bad choices and wandered.

Sometimes when our children go astray we forget about the truths of God that have been planted in their lives. These are the crucial seeds of God that may lie dormant for a long while, but they are seeds from the eternal Sower that will find root in His time. Heartbroken parents may gain comfort and hope in knowing that their prayers are heard and their tears are collected in His bottle.

His pride hurt but not yet conquered, the prodigal son descended one step lower into disgrace. He took a job feeding swine, animals considered an abomination in Israel. Then the Lord worked His miracle—the boy "came to his senses." What a wonderful statement! Now in his right mind, he came to the conclusion that he could return to his father's house and work as a servant. His new humility granted him no presumption that his father would ever accept him as a son again, but at least his father's servants were fed. With food he would have been content.

We know the rest of the story. *Home* is a wonderfully consoling word. How dear it must have seemed to that son whose heart had been quickened. How sorrowful he must have felt when he thought about his last encounter with his father. What shame he carried as he envisioned himself as a beggar at their reunion.

Even as a father and mother today have wept bitter tears in prayer and have waited for the return of a child, so this father had waited. He had waited in anticipation of his son's return, for he saw him from a distance and did not wait for his knock on the door but ran to meet his wayward child. This son, renewed and humbled, returned home to the open arms of a loving father.

Another famous wanderer was a gifted orator who received an excellent education at the best schools of his time. This son fell among bad companions and was led astray into deep sin. As a young man of eighteen, he began a relationship with a woman with whom he lived, unmarried, for thirteen years. He also involved himself in various heretical teachings, creating an even greater distance from his Christian upbringing.

His mother and her fervent prayers to God on his behalf chased him for years—through his corrupt behavior and his heresies. When the young man, Augustine, was age thirty-three, wearied after years spent searching for satisfaction of heart and the meaning of life in all the wrong places, the words of Romans 13:13–14 quickened his heart to a new birth: "Let us walk properly, as in the day, not in revelry and drunkenness, not in lewdness and lust, not in strife and envy. But put on the Lord Jesus Christ, and make no provision for the flesh, to fulfill its lusts" (NKJV).

Saint Augustine lived to become one of the great fathers and theologians of the church. There is always hope for those who have strayed, even among the most defiled.

How many parents have agonized over their children and how many, like Saint Augustine's mother, Monica, have witnessed the return of those loved ones. To surrender our children to the Lord and to commit ourselves to weep and pray for them are mighty weapons for their defense.

God works in the hearts of our children, though we sometimes can't see the results of that work. Often it is the full surrender of a child that enables God to perform His work effectively. Surrender is not easy, and frequently it involves a lot of pain—for the child as well as the parent.

Because of our love for them, we want our children's lives to be poured out liberally and profusely for the right things. God loves them much more than we can, for He loves them in all purity and righteousness. While we struggle through this valley of frustration and uncertainty, no matter how deep, He will uphold us with His arms and follow our children with His eye.

Lord, help us to surrender the fears
in our hearts over our children to You.
We pray for wisdom as we seek
to handle the difficult times in their lives.
We surrender them into Your loving arms.

The Lord
Is the Lifter
of My Head

But thou, O Lord,
art a shield about me,
my glory, and the
lifter of my head.

PSALM 3:3 RSV

19

DIVORCE

Abide with me; fast falls the eventide,
The darkness deepens; Lord, with me abide.
When other helpers fail and comforts flee,
Help of the helpless, O abide with me.
(HENRY F. LYTE)

As I look back over the last twenty-one years, I realize how abundantly blessed I have been. Those twenty-one years could have been very different for my husband and me if the Lord had not intervened in our lives. At a time of crisis in our marriage, we were miraculously saved by His mercy and grace. The crisis was the means that God used to open our eyes to the destitution of our souls as well as our relationship.

I will forever be thankful for that interruption of life for us, though very painful, because we became born again to the Lord and to each other. I realize we could have become just another statistic in the growing number of divorce cases, but God showed us overflowing mercy. In the years that have followed, He has helped us repair and rebuild that which had been so damaged.

Many others have not been so fortunate. Probably most of us have family members or close friends who have been through the valley of divorce. This is a deep and sad place for all involved—not only the husband and wife but children, especially, and extended family members. All become victims of the great enemy of our souls, Satan. The result is a "living death," a union of two that has now been severed but without the funeral and burial.

It is alarming to know that according to some figures the percentage of divorce within the church has now exceeded that of the non-Christian world. Some of the words of a song say, "What's too painful to remember, we simply choose to forget." Ask anyone who has been through the pain of divorce and see if he or she has been able to erase the damage inflicted by this severance. The Hebrew root of the word *divorce* means "to put away," but it also implies the severing of a living union, a kind of amputation. Since God created marriage for the union of two people to become one, the separating of that union is, indeed, like an amputation.

The right and wrong of divorce is not the subject to be addressed in this chapter. The cause, the fault, the repercussions are not the focus. Those who have been involved in this all-too-frequent scenario are well aware of the bitter roots that brought forth the fruit of divorce. The main thought here is to offer hope to those whose hearts have been bruised and shattered, to encourage them to look to the solace of heaven for healing.

One woman who found this hope was familiar with our topic. We can learn of her story in the Bible in John 4:4–32. She was called merely a "Samaritan woman," or the "woman at the well." John relates her glorious encounter with the Savior and His wonderful gift to her.

Jesus and His disciples were traveling through Samaria and came near a city called Sychar. Jesus was tired from the journey and stopped to rest at Jacob's well at noon. His disciples went into the city to buy food. The Samaritan woman also came to the well to draw water at that time for she knew there would be few people there.

I can imagine that this woman, after numerous marriages and at least one immoral relationship, had a wretched reputation among her own people. I doubt if she had many friends. I can picture her as being defensive on the outside but bereft and fragile on the inside. The hopelessness of her life, I am sure, made her shoulders stoop. What a touching picture of someone whose life was passing by in despair—after having five husbands, she was obviously no longer a young woman. Her past was soiled and filled with shame; her future held no promise, and her present was depressing.

How like the Lord to be touched with the sadness of such a one. When Jesus spoke to her, she was astounded—men, especially rabbis, did not address women in public, and Jews did not associate with Samaritans at all. For Him to ask a drink of water from her, a woman, a tainted woman at that, and a Samaritan, was amazing. She answered Jesus with those thoughts in mind, "How can you ask me for a drink?"

His response was simple. He offered Himself, the hope of life, to her, though she did not yet understand. "If you knew the gift of God and who it is that asks you for a drink, you would have asked him and he would have given you living water" (John 4:10). The woman obviously was aware there was something different about this particular Jew, and she knew He was touching on something of a spiritual nature when she asked Him if He was "greater than our father Jacob" (verse 12).

Jesus continued to drive His point home regarding the living water as He pointed out that drinking this water she would never thirst again. She immediately desired this water, but apparently for physical reasons—so that she wouldn't get thirsty and have to keep returning to the well to draw more water. Jesus proceeded to open her darkened mind to the truth as He revealed His knowledge of her past. "Go, call your husband and come back" (verse 16). Shame must have engulfed her whole being when she had to admit she had no husband.

Yet Jesus did not chide her. He did not break a bruised reed. He continued to fan the fire of enlightenment in her soul. The Lord opened her heart to understanding as she acknowledged Him to be a prophet and began to ask Him about the form of worship. He explained that neither the place nor the form was of consequence—it was the posture of the heart, for true worshipers must worship God in spirit and in truth. The woman had heard about the Messiah's coming and told Jesus so. Jesus' confession to this poor outcast that He is the Messiah must have left her overcome with joy, for she left her water jar and ran to give testimony of the Savior to the people of her village.

As a result of her conversion and witness, many other Samaritans were led to believe in the Lord Jesus. Again we see the Lord using one whose life seemed irreparable to show forth the great depth of His mercy.

I'm sure this woman of Samaria was once again able to hold her head high. She was now a member of God's royal family. Her life, from the moment of her conversion, changed. She would never be the same again, and others would see that transformation in her life. She had found in Christ what she had been looking for all her life—someone to love her unconditionally. She would remember her sins from time to time and still suffer consequences, but the Lord would not bring the subject of her past up again. He had set her free.

Many have gone through heartbreaking situations beyond their control. They never sought nor wanted divorce but did not have a choice. They suffer from a decision that was forced upon them. Others suffer from deep feelings of guilt from the wrong choices they have made themselves that have resulted in a broken marriage. Many have had to make tough judgments because of physical danger for themselves or their children.

More, I am convinced, live in a state of divorce without the legal documentation—living together physically yet millions of miles apart in every other way. They have never grown together and so have grown apart. Theirs is not a separation of address but a divorce of heart and mind, and the result is nonetheless a tragedy. Different situations, yet the same outcome. All suffer.

We know that God hates divorce. We also know He is a healer of soul and spirit. The Samaritan woman, for whatever reasons she chose to marry five times, found healing in the balm of the Lord's grace. Whatever your circumstances may be or may have been, if you are one of these victims, you too may find that precious comfort and protection in the refuge of the Redeemer's arms.

*Father, may we understand
with all our hearts that Your grace is
deeper than all our sins,
Your love gives comfort to the brokenhearted,
and Your strength is sufficient
for all our circumstances.*

God Is
My Comfort

*Praise be to the God and Father
of our Lord Jesus Christ,
the Father of compassion
and the God of all comfort,
who comforts us in all our troubles,
so that we can comfort those
in any trouble with the comfort
we ourselves have received from God.*

— 2 CORINTHIANS 1:3—4

20

DEATH OF A CHILD

*You had no fear, did you, my child,
when the angels appeared at your door,
to transport you home on the wings of the morn
to the treasures Heaven has in store?*

$\mathcal{M}$y sister Becky and her husband anticipated this moment for a long time and tried to prepare for the appointment as best they could. When the occasion arrived, and they were faced with the awful reality of the death of their oldest daughter, nothing could have readied them for the grief it brought.

They lived for almost twenty-five years with the knowledge of that impending fate, for Beth had been diagnosed as an infant with an incurable disease. Those years were spent in and out of hospitals, with innumerable tests, constant medication, and near-death experiences. Beth survived the probable age expectancy of her disease—by God's grace and the determination He seemed to have instilled in her—by several years.

My niece was an inspiration to others—her family, friends, doctors, and hospital staff. Although she knew her condition was grave, she never let it overcome her resolve to rise above it. She insisted on being treated as a normal person, whether in school, at home, or when she was involved in the activities of her cousins. One of the highlights of her life was her high school graduation.

During the latter part of her life, she had part of one leg amputated, then part of her other foot due to complications from the disease. However, with the help of a prosthesis, she still maintained most of her activities. All of the family knew that without a miracle from God, her prognosis for prolonged life expectancy was not good. The strain and agony for her parents and her younger sister during that period seemed insurmountable at times.

It is an agonizing thing to watch one of your children suffer under any circumstance, but one of the most devastating trials of life is to lose a child. It is not the usual sequence of events for a child to precede parents in this date that all must face. Whether it is a child not yet born or one who has been taken suddenly in infancy, whether it is a child with an illness, like Beth, or whether death is a result of some accident, whether a child is young or older makes little difference—this tragedy is one of the deepest valleys a parent could ever encounter.

Another mother long ago anguished at the death of her son. There was no bed where he could lie, nor could she cradle his head in his dying moments, speaking tender words of love to him. What thoughts must have gone through her mind! Did she remember the struggle of bearing her first child, hearing the first sound of his small cry, and then, with joy, cuddling him to her breast? Did she think of his years as a boy, learning to work with his hands as a carpenter? Was her heart pierced with pain when she recalled the time his family could not find him, only to discover he was doing his Father's work, amazing the religious leaders with his knowledge? Did she wonder at the ministry of this young man who worked signs and miracles? Did she think of the angel Gabriel who announced his coming birth, or the shepherds who were the first to pay him tribute? As she pondered these things, did she recall that she had been told that "a sword will pierce your own soul too"? Would she remember that this child had been called the Son of the Most High?

This Son's Father watched also. And His heart broke as His only Son took the sin and shame and guilt of all sons and daughters of the earth. His precious and perfect Son, who had never known separation from Him, now took upon Himself the death that all humans deserved in order that they might have life with Him. This Son endured that shame for the "joy set before him." He knew that His work on earth was completed and He would rejoin His heavenly Father at His right hand.

God understands the anguish when a child dies. The hollow that grief bores into the heart may be filled with the abundance of His comfort. He loved us enough to give His only Son to die in order that sin, which causes death, might be forever conquered.

In the difficulty of trusting God and His purposes when a tragedy like this occurs, allow Him to use even the pain to bring glory to Himself and to minister through your pain to others who are undergoing similar circumstances. Even in her suffering, Beth became a minister of the grace of God to those around her. The frustration she experienced so often because of illness finally became the surrender of her heart. God clothed her with His peace, and, ultimately, the Lord she came to love more than her life used her condition to be a channel of peace to others.

In the same way, my sister has been able to comfort others who are going through deep waters of sorrow. And as a result of watching her older sister go through many difficult times in the hospital, my niece Bonnie has become an occupational therapist, compassionately helping others as Beth had been helped.

We struggle in this life with so many uncertainties. We are never assured of anything except God Himself; He is the one constant, unchangeable element in all things, the hope of all who trust in Him. We can find comfort in our loving God and lie upon His breast with our tears and sorrows. The sorrow may remain for a season, but there is enduring comfort from One who is our hope beyond this life. For the believer, that hope in Christ will one day be realized.

God of all comfort, enable us through our grief
to lean upon the arms of Christ. When words cannot
be uttered, be our voice; when strength is depleted,
be our refuge; when hope wavers, be our vision.
May the Giver of life restore our hearts in You.

God Is
the Strength
of My Heart

*My flesh and my heart may fail,
but God is the strength of my heart
and my portion forever.*

PSALM 73:26

21

DEATH OF A SPOUSE

There are times when my heart is heavy,
And this earthen vessel feels its clay.
I pause, then, amid the noise of life;
I think of you, and smile.

A few years ago my husband and I sat at the funeral service of a loved one, one who was a husband and a father. The service was a wonderful memorial celebration of a dear man who had suffered a long time and was now at rest with his Maker. During the service, I looked around at those in attendance. As I gazed at the sad smiles, the tear-stained faces, my heart was stabbed with the realization that someday either my husband or I would, of necessity, go through this ceremony, unless Christ returns first or we die at the same time. The thought was painful, and the lump in my throat swelled as I tried to swallow the impression brought to my mind.

This topic is the last subject I have detailed in this book. I have purposely left it until last because it has not been something pleasant for me to consider and is probably the most emotionally difficult to write. Five years ago when the inspiration for this book idea surfaced in my heart, I began writing on some of the topics. When I came to the theme at hand, I found that my heart failed me for the anguish it created deep within. I had to put it aside.

I have contemplated this chapter for months, even years now. As I begin to address this particular valley of sorrow, I realize the peace that God has brought to my heart over this period of time. It is still not pleasing to encounter, yet it is no longer as affecting as it once was. In the depth of love that God has grown within me for my husband, I know each day together is a precious gift from Him. Though things are not always smooth, things are always bearable because we have each other. And because we have been blessed with this gift, the future, whatever it may bring, will always be blessed with the memory of that enduring love.

Even though we know as believers our hope is in Christ and our reunions in heaven will be sweet, the grief is still very real. The prospect of losing one dearest to your heart is a somber, almost unbearable thought.

The great Christian philosopher and writer C. S. Lewis found this to be true when, late in his life, love came to him very unexpectedly.

During a time of great disillusionment, a young mother with two small children was introduced to the writings of C. S. Lewis (who was known as Jack to his friends). A Jewish woman who had renounced her religion in favor of communism, Joy was married to an alcoholic, abuser, and adulterer, and her life seemed to have bottomed out.

As so often is the case, God had placed Joy in such a position of hopelessness so that she had no one to whom she could turn but Him. Of her conversion, she later wrote that she was the world's "most astonished atheist."

Joy Gresham was also a writer. She was encouraged by a publishing friend to write to C. S. Lewis, whose works had so affected her. To her surprise, her letter to him started a regular correspondence between the two.

During the course of time, her husband demanded a divorce from her to marry another woman. With reluctance because of her Christian convictions, Joy agreed. Notwithstanding all her personal tragedy, she had finally met Jack Lewis, and their casual friendship began to develop into something deeper. She moved from New York to England with her two sons to begin a new life.

When the time came for her visitor's visa to be renewed, Joy faced the crisis of having to return to America. In a strange development, for the purposes of practicality —at least from Jack's perspective—he decided to marry Joy to enable her to remain in London. The marriage was a mere formality, and she remained "Mrs. Gresham."

This formality, however, evolved into much more. God would take the heartbreak of illness to fan the flames of love. Within a few months of their civil service ceremony, Joy was diagnosed with bone cancer. She was not given long to live because of the advanced stage of the disease, so Jack called a minister in to the hospital, and he and Joy were married in a Christian ceremony, Jack beside his bride in her hospital bed, each poignantly reciting "for richer, for poorer; in sickness and in health." Tragedy had found its mark in Jack's heart, and friendship became love.

That love deepened, as did the pain of watching Joy

suffer. The disease went into a state of remission for a while, and they were enabled to have a few years of happiness together. Each of them was resigned to the likelihood of the recurrence of the cancer, and they relished each new day the Lord gave to them.

Of course, the cancer did return, and Joy died, her husband at her bedside. Well aware of what was happening, she told Jack how happy he had made her and that she was at peace with God. With that, she died with a smile on her lips, but Jack realized her smile was for some unseen Person in the room.

He faced tremendous battles with grief over the next several months, unable to fully accept his great loss. In time, by writing out his feelings of despondency, he came to understand that his immense bereavement was selfish. His grief had masked the realization that Joy had been set free from her pain and the sentence of death that had hung over her for so long. In this way, God helped him overcome his despair.

His "autumn" love had blossomed like the springtime and was over, it seemed, just as quickly. Jack described their marriage as one ship. "The ship of their love had had a rough passage through cruel seas. The storms were over, but they had taken their toll: 'The starboard engine has gone. I, the port engine, must chug along somehow till we make harbour. . . .'"[1]

It is a beautiful late autumn day—crisp and clear—as I begin writing this chapter. I sit outside in a quiet, calm setting, meditating on the brevity of life, not in a somber way but more in a realistic attitude. I am sitting among many people whom I do not know, yet it is very peaceful. The gentle wind is cool, and golden leaves tumble quietly to the ground, creating a floor of sunshine. Though I am encompassed by many, it is quite lonely, and I have found it is a good place to meet with the Lord.

I look out across the landscape and view the many headstones around me, very conscious that most of those lying beneath the stones were someone's wife or husband in life. I sit in the middle of a cemetery where I have wept much and prayed much as I have walked amid the graves. I have wept because I have come to realize that sin is a great robber of life and its golden crown is death. For those whose lives have become one, the theft is irreplaceable. God ordained marriage to be so sacred that He compares it to the relationship of Christ to His church. When the union of marriage is broken by death, the remaining partner has lost a part of him- or herself.

It is raining lightly as I continue the second day of my journey through this chapter. I have found writing on this subject amid the quiet of the setting to be a very pleasant way to meditate on the Lord. I think the epitaphs written upon headstones indicate something of a person's life and wonder what my family would inscribe for me. As these thoughts occur to me, I think of Christians referring to a departed loved one as having "gone home to be with the Lord." This place is a solemn reminder that we are pilgrims here on this earth. Our hope is not in this life but in eternity. That gives great comfort and peace.

The rustle of the leaves adds to the beauty of the song of the wind chimes. I am so aware that all creation praises

God, in life or in death. I sit before a headstone that eloquently speaks of His glory. "I am the resurrection and the life. He who believes in Me, though he may die, he shall live. And whoever lives and believes in Me shall never die" (John 11:25–26 NKJV).

Someday on life's horizon, one of us will stand beside an open grave of the other with the unutterable sadness of saying a final good-bye. But each tear that may fall is saturated with the promise of reunion in heaven. Each sigh of grief will be replaced with the unspeakable joy of reigning, side by side, together with Christ forever. We grieve not in vain. What death has stolen will be replaced immeasurably by the good hand of our King.

When the trumpet of the Lord shall sound,
And time shall be no more,
And the morning breaks, eternal, bright and fair;
When the saved of earth shall gather over on the other shore,
And the roll is called up yonder, I'll be there.

(JAMES M. BLACK)

NOTE

1. Brian Sibley, *C. S. Lewis Through the Shadowlands: The Story of His Life with Joy Davidman,* 2d ed. (Grand Rapids: Revell, 1994), 167.

CLOSING COMMENTS

$\mathcal{T}$he psalmist said, "My soul is weary with sorrow; strengthen me according to your word" (Psalm 119:28). The Bible is full of comforting and encouraging verses indicating God's relationship to the believer, especially in the book of Psalms. That is why each topic in this book begins with one of these verses—they direct our thoughts to our true Consolation. The Bible also gives us wonderful examples of people in all walks of life who have traveled through the same valleys that we journey today. I hope this will bring encouragement to the reader.

God's Word is powerful, and it is relevant to each area of life, regardless of the time or place or circumstance. I have endeavored in this book to help people focus on this eternal truth. The Lord doesn't always eliminate our problems, but He strengthens us *through* them, leading us with a careful and tender eye. There is a tremendous surety in His Word. It is always dependable and steadfast. The foundation never wavers because it is Christ Himself.

It is my prayer that God will use this book to bring encouragement and hope to hurting hearts and to heal the wounds inflicted by life's passage by looking to the Keeper of our souls. This is the same Lord who says,

They were glad when it grew calm, and
he guided them to their desired haven.
Let them give thanks to the LORD for his unfailing love.

(PSALM 107:30–31)

Moody Press, a ministry of Moody Bible Institute,
is designed for education, evangelization, and edification.
If we may assist you in knowing more about Christ
and the Christian life, please write us without obligation:
Moody Press, c/o MLM, Chicago, Illinois 60610.